New York Interiors
Intérieurs new-yorkais

Beate Wedekind

Edited by | Herausgegeben von | Sous la direction de
Angelika Taschen

New York Interiors
Intérieurs new-yorkais

TASCHEN

KÖLN LONDON LOS ANGELES MADRID PARIS TOKYO

llustration page 2 / Abbildung Seite 2 / Reproduction page 2:
Detail of the living room of David McDermott and Peter McGough
Detail des Wohnraumes von David McDermott und Peter McGough
Détail de la salle de séjour de David McDermott et Peter McGough
Photo: Pieter Estersohn

Illustration page 7 / Abbildung Seite 7 / Reproduction page 7:
Map of New York City
Stadtplan von New York City
Plan de New York City
Drawing: Alberto Berengo Gardin

Endpaper / Vorsatzpapier / Pages de garde:
Aerial view of New York City
Luftansicht von New York City
Vue aérienne de New York City
Photo: Richard Laird / FPG International Corp.

Front cover / Umschlagvorderseite / Couverture:
The kitchen/eating area of Michèle Oka Doner
Der Küchen- und Essbereich von Michèle Oka Doner
Le coin cuisine/repas de Michèle Oka Doner
Photo: Todd Eberle

Back cover / Umschlagrückseite / Dos de couverture:
New York from above
New York von oben
New York vu d'en haut
Photo: Getty Images

© 2002 TASCHEN GmbH
Hohenzollernring 53, D-50672 Köln
www.taschen.com
Conception and design by Angelika Taschen, Cologne
Text edited by Jutta Hendricks, Susanne Klinkhamels and Angelika Taschen, Cologne
Photographic co-ordination by Trixi Schaumberger and Letitia Ord (Assistant), New York
Cover design by Angelika Taschen, Cologne
French translation by Thérèse Chatelain-Südkamp, Cologne (pp. 28–175),
and Michèle Schreyer, Cologne (pp. 8–27, pp. 176–300)
English translation by Almut Fitzgerald, Riverdale (NY)
German translation by Gabriele-Sabine Gugetzer, Hamburg (pp. 20–25)

Printed in Italy
ISBN 3-8228-1872-0

Contents
Inhalt
Sommaire

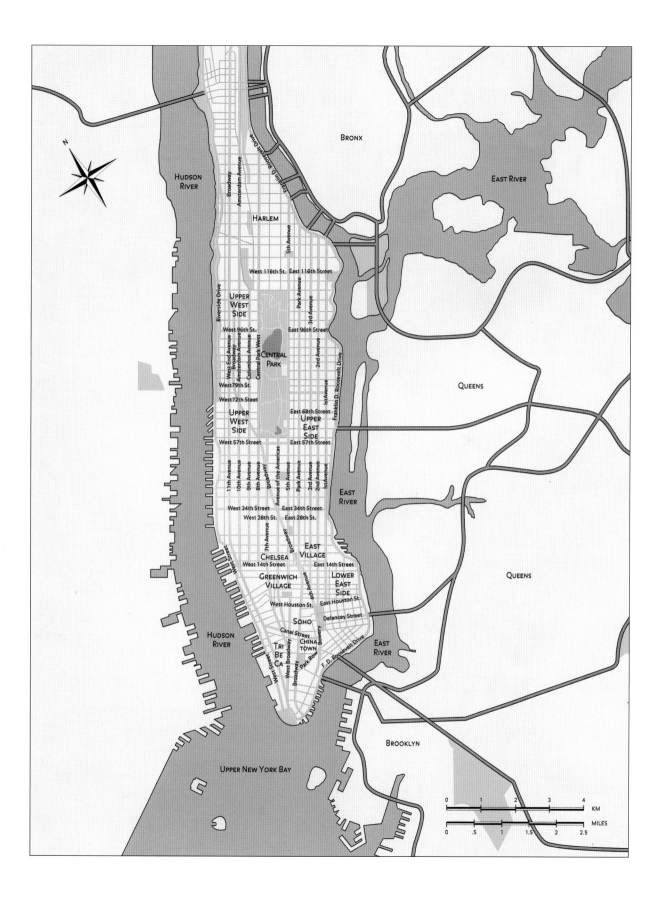

N

HUDSON
RIVER

BRONX

EAST RIVER

Broadway
Amsterdam Avenue
Edgar D. Roosevelt Drive

HARLEM

5th Avenue

West 116th St.   East 116th Street

Riverside Drive

UPPER
WEST
SIDE

Park Avenue
3rd Avenue

West 96th St.   East 96th Street

West End Avenue
Broadway
Amsterdam Avenue
Columbus Avenue
Central Park West

CENTRAL
PARK

2nd Avenue

West 79th St.

West 72th Steet

1st Avenue
Franklin D. Roosevelt Drive

UPPER
WEST
SIDE

East 68th Street

UPPER
EAST
SIDE

QUEENS

West 57th Street   East 57th Street

11th Avenue
10th Avenue
9th Avenue
8th Avenue
Broadway
Avenue of the Americas
5th Avenue
Park Avenue
3rd Avenue
2nd Avenue
1st Avenue

EAST
RIVER

West 34th Street   East 34th Street

West 28th St.   East 28th St.

7th Avenue
Broadway

EAST
VILLAGE

QUEENS

West Street

CHELSEA

West 14th Street   East 14th Street

GREENWICH
VILLAGE

LOWER
EAST
SIDE

9th Avenue

West Houston St.   East Houston St.

SOHO

Delancey Street

West Street

Canal Street

TRI
BE
CA

West Broadway

CHINA
TOWN

Broadway
Park Row

Bowery

F. D. Roosevelt Drive

EAST
RIVER

HUDSON
RIVER

BROOKLYN

UPPER NEW YORK BAY

0   1   2   3   4   KM

MILES

0   .5   1   1.5   2   2.5

New York City

Manhattan, home for all the world's cultures, is a cosmos in itself, an island about 21 km long and 3 km wide, between the Hudson and the East River. There are five boroughs of the City of New York: Manhattan, the Bronx, Brooklyn, Queens, and Staten Island, and the smallest of them is Manhattan. Worldwide, some of Manhattan's districts are synonymous with New York, such as the Financial District, Chinatown, Little Italy, TriBeCa, the Lower East Side, SoHo, Greenwich Village, Midtown, the Upper West Side, the Upper East Side, Central Park, and Harlem. Its famous skyline of skyscrapers has made Manhattan into a symbol of America, standing for power and money, the essential metropolis. With Wall Street, the World Trade Center and Fifth Avenue, Manhattan is the center of the international business world; with the Lincoln Center, the Metropolitan Opera, the Museum of Modern Art, Carnegie Hall, Madison Square Garden, Broadway, and Times Square, Manhattan has the most renowned cultural and entertainment centers; it's the seat of the United Nations and the hub of countless major international corporations. Manhattan is an island of superlatives: the Empire State Building, built in 1931 and 102 storeys high, is the world's best known building. More multimillionaires have a residence on the elegant streets of Manhattan's Upper East Side than anywhere else on the globe. People from more than 100 nations live in New York and 121 languages are spoken. Interesting people of many sorts have always called Manhattan their home – from Enrico Caruso, Igor Stravinsky and Leonard Bernstein, through Al Capone and Meyer Lansky, to Jacqueline Kennedy-Onassis, Andy Warhol, and the New York stars of today, such as Woody Allen, Barbra Streisand, Madonna, Placido Domingo, Calvin Klein and Donna Karan.

Manhattan ist ein Kosmos für sich, eine 21 km lange und 3 km schmale Insel zwischen Hudson und East River, in dem die Kulturen der Welt ihre Heimat gefunden haben. Der kleinste der fünf Distrikte von New York City (Manhattan, Bronx, Brooklyn, Queens, Staten Islands) beherbergt die Stadtteile, die überall auf der Welt Synonym für New York sind: Financial District, Chinatown, Little Italy, TriBeCa, Lower East Side, SoHo, Greenwich Village, Midtown, Upper West Side, Upper East Side, Central Park, Harlem. Seine berühmte Wolkenkratzer-Skyline macht Manhattan zum Symbol Amerikas, für Macht und Geld, zur Metropole per se. Manhattan ist Zentrum der internationalen Geschäftswelt (unter anderem Wallstreet, World Trade Center, Fifth Avenue), der renommiertesten Kultur- und Entertainment-Institutionen (unter anderem Lincoln Center, Metropolitan Opera, Museum of Modern Art, Carnegie Hall, Madison Square Garden, Broadway, Times Square, Sitz der Vereinten Nationen, zahlloser Zentralen der wichtigsten Konzerne der Welt. Manhattan ist eine Insel der Superlative: Das 1931 fertiggestellte, 102 Stockwerke hohe Empire State Building ist das bekannteste Gebäude der Welt. In den eleganten Straßen der Upper East Side Manhattans wohnen mehr Multimillionäre als irgendwo sonst. In New York leben Menschen aus über 100 Nationen, werden 121 Sprachen gesprochen. Und schon immer haben interessante Zeitgenossen jeglicher Couleur Manhattan ihre Heimat genannt. Von Enrico Caruso, Igor Strawinsky, Leonard Bernstein über Al Capone und ;Meyer Lansky, Jacqueline Kennedy-Onassis und Andy Warhol bis zu den New-York-Stars von heute, wie Woody Allen und Barbra Streisand, Madonna und Placido Domingo, Calvin Klein und Donna Karan.

Manhattan est un univers en soi, une île étroite de 21 kilomètres de long sur 3 kilomètres de large entre le Hudson et la East-River, dans laquelle les cultures du monde entier ont trouvé une patrie. Le plus petit des cinq districts de New York (Manhattan, Bronx, Brooklyn, Queens, Staten Islands) réunit les quartiers que le monde entier considère comme le véritable New York: Financial Districts, China Town, Little Italy, TriBeCa, Lower East Side, SoHo, Greenwich Village, Midtown, Upper West Side, Upper East Side, Central Park, Harlem. Ses célèbres gratte-ciel font de Manhattan le symbole de l'Amérique, symbole de pouvoir et d'argent, de métropole. Manhattan est le centre international des affaires (entre autres Wallstreet, World Trade Center, Fifth Avenue), des institutions renommées de la culture et du spectacle (entre autres Lincoln Center, Metropolitan Opera, Museum of Modern Art, Carnegie Hall, Madison Square Garden, Broadway, Time Square), le siège des Nations unies, c'est là que se trouvent les innombrables bureaux des groupes les plus importants du monde. Manhattan est une île des superlatifs: l'Empire State Building de 102 étages, construit en 1931, est le bâtiment le plus célèbre du monde. Dans les rues élégantes de la Upper East Side de Manhattan habitent plus de multimillionnaires que nulle part ailleurs. A New York vivent des gens originaires de plus de cent nations, on y parle 121 langues. Et depuis toujours, des personnalités intéressantes de tous bords ont choisi de vivre à Manhattan. D'Enrico Caruso, Igor Stravinsky, Leonard Bernstein, en passant par Al Capone et Meyer Lansky, Jacqueline Kennedy-Onassis et Andy Warhol aux stars new-yorkaises de notre temps comme Woody Allen et Barbra Streisand, Madonna et Placido Domingo, Calvin Klein et Donna Karan.

C'est au cœur de la colonie d'artistes TriBeCa (Triangle Below Canal) que sont situés les bâtiments d'une petite usine désaffectée où vit l'artiste français Arman avec sa femme Corice et leurs enfants. Les quatre niveaux de l'ancienne fabrique de mixed pickles font chacun d'environ 350 m² et sont reliés par un monte-charge. Au rez-de-chaussée se trouvent l'atelier d'Arman et le garage, au premier la chambre d'enfants et la chambre d'amis, au second le salon, la salle à manger et la cuisine, et au troisième la chambre d'Arman et de Corice. A partir des étages supérieurs la vue sur l'Hudson est fantastique. Les collections d'Arman – sculptures africaines et armures japonaises – ainsi que ses propres assemblages remplissent toute la maison. Maître du Nouveau Réalisme, il rassemble les objets les plus courants comme les plus extraordinaires pour les intégrer dans son art. Lorsqu'Arman arriva pour la première fois à New York en 1963, il sut tout de suite qu'il aimerait y vivre. Si les rues couvertes d'ordures en contrarient plus d'un, elles ne cessent de remplir d'allégresse son âme de chiffonnier.

Arman

For the French artist Arman, home is a narrow loft building in the heart of the artists colony TriBeCa (Triangle Below Canal), where he lives with his wife Corice and their children in a former pickle factory. Each of the four floors has an area of about 350 sq.m. The first floor is Arman's studio, the second is for the children and guests, the third is divided into a living room, dining room and kitchen, while the fourth floor is the sleeping area. The upper storeys offer a striking view of the Hudson River. The entire house is filled with Arman's collections. In every nook and cranny are African sculptures, Japanese armor or his own assemblage art. A master of New Realism, he is a passionate collector of household artifacts, which he incorporates into his creations. In 1963, when Arman first came to New York, he knew this was his city. Refuse piled up on the sidewalks may be an eyesore for many, but for Arman, an avid collector of junk, it was Eldorado.

Im Herzen der Künstler-Kolonie TriBeCa (Triangle Below Canal) liegt das schmale Industriegebäude, in dem der französische Künstler Arman mit seiner Frau Corice und den Kindern lebt. Jedes der vier Stockwerke der ehemaligen Mixed-Pickles-Fabrik umfaßt circa 350 m² Wohnfläche. Sie sind durch einen Lastenaufzug miteinander verbunden: Im Parterre befinden sich Armans Atelier und eine Garage, im ersten Stock Kinder- und Gästezimmer, im zweiten Salon, Eßzimmer, Küche und im dritten Stock der Schlafbereich von Arman und Corice. Von den oberen Etagen hat man einen phantastischen Blick über den Hudson River. Das ganze Haus ist bis in den kleinsten Winkel gefüllt mit Armans Sammlungen afrikanischer Skulpturen und japanischer Rüstungen sowie seiner eigenen Assemblage-Kunst. Der Künstler sammelt wie besessen einfache und ungewöhnliche Gebrauchsgegenstände und integriert sie in seine Kunstwerke. Als Arman 1963 das erste Mal nach New York kam, war ihm sofort klar, daß dies seine Stadt ist. Der Straßenmüll – für andere ein Ärgernis sondergleichen – läßt seitdem sein Sammlerherz jubeln.

Première page: le salon. Au-dessus de la cheminée, «Les Mousquetaires» d'Arman, 1962. Devant, les boîtes Brillo d'Andy Warhol.
Ci-dessus: «Persistance des impressions», tel est le nom de l'œuvre réalisée en 1991 par Arman avec des lampes de bureau anglaises. A gauche, une statue Dogon en bois originaire du Mali; au premier plan, des armures Yoroï du Japon.
A droite: dans l'entrée, un banc de Gaudí.
Page de droite: Au-dessus du buffet Regency les «Eight Guitars» d'Arman dominent la pièce du salon. Les chaises en forme de violon, les tables et les objets en porcelaine sont également de lui.

First page: the drawing room. Above the fireplace is Arman's "Les Mousquetaires", 1962, in the foreground Andy Warhol's Brillo Boxes.
Above: "Persistance des impressions" is Arman's 1991 creation made from English desk lamps. On the left is a Dogon wood sculpture from Mali, in the foreground Japanese Yoroï armors.
Right: At the entrance is a bench by Gaudí.
Facing page: The dining room is dominated by Arman's "Eight Guitars", which hangs above an English Regency sideboard. Violin-shaped chairs, tables and china objects are also by Arman.

Erste Seite: Blick in den Salon. Über dem Kamin Armans »Les Mousquetaires« von 1962. Vorne die Brillo-Boxes von Andy Warhol.
Oben: »Persistance des impressions« heißt das 1991 entstandene Werk Armans aus englischen Schreibtischlampen. Links eine Dogon-Holzstatue aus Mali, davor zwei japanische Yoroï-Rüstungen.
Rechts: im Eingang eine Bank von Gaudí.
Rechte Seite: Das Eßzimmer beherrschen »Eight Guitars« von Arman über dem englischen Regency-Sideboard. Violinförmige Stühle, Tische und die Porzellanobjekte sind ebenfalls sein Werk.

Lorsque Brooke Astor, l'épouse de Vincent Astor, devint veuve en
1959, elle héritait d'une des plus grosses fortunes du monde. Son mari
lui léguait en outre la Fondation Vincent-Astor, qu'elle préside active-
ment, et les projets sociaux et culturels dont le soutien financier
s'élève jusqu'ici à plus de 200 millions de dollars. Fondation et projets
sont établis exclusivement à New York. Venu de Waldorf dans la
Hesse, l'arrière-arrière-grand-père John Jacob Astor arriva à New York
avec 1 dollar en poche. Quand il y mourut en 1848, il était devenu
l'homme le plus riche d'Amérique. Née en 1902, Brooke Astor, encore
vive et alerte, est la doyenne de la société américaine. Elle a reçu
toutes les personnalités importantes du monde entier dans ses deux
appartements du 15e et 16e étage, situés sur la Park Avenue dans la
Upper East Side. Presque tous les soirs, elle invite à dîner. Dans le
salon décoré par Parish Hadley au début des années 80, l'ambiance
est détendue. Les chiens cavalent sur les vieux tapis et Mrs Vincent
Astor bavarde sans arrêt au téléphone.

Brooke Astor

In 1959, when Brooke Astor's husband Vincent died, she became
one of the richest women in the world. At present she is acting
president of his legacy, the Vincent Astor Foundation. So far, the
foundation has donated more than 200 million dollars for social
and cultural projects, in New York alone. In 1783, Brooke Astor's
great-great-grandfather John Jacob Astor arrived in New York from
the Hessian town of Waldorf with just one dollar in his pocket. In
1848, he died the wealthiest man in America. Brooke Astor, born in
1902, is still the dynamic and spirited grande dame. The doyenne
of American society has hosted every illustrious name in the world.
A fascinating group of guests dines regularly in her Park Avenue
duplex, whose drawing rooms were decorated by Parish Hadley in
the early 80s. The mood is relaxed, and dogs play on the priceless
carpets as Mrs Astor makes yet another telephone call.

Als Mrs Vincent Astor 1959 Witwe wurde, hinterließ ihr Mann eines
der größten Vermögen der Welt – und die Vincent-Astor-Stiftung, der
Brooke Astor aktiv vorsteht. Bisher hat sie mit über 200 Millionen
Dollar soziale und kulturelle Projekte ausschließlich in New York un-
terstützt. Ururgroßvater John Jacob Astor kam 1783 mit einem Dollar
in der Westentasche aus dem hessischen Waldorf nach New York und
starb dort 1848 als reichster Mann Amerikas. Brooke Astor, 1902 geboren, hellwach und agil, ist die Doyenne der amerikanischen Gesell-
schaft. In ihren beiden Apartments im 15. und 16. Stock an der Upper
East Side der Park Avenue waren alle wichtigen Zeitgenossen der
Welt zu Gast. Fast jeden Abend lädt sie zum Dinner ein. Die Atmosphäre in den von Parish Hadley Anfang der 80er Jahre dekorierten
Salons ist leger. Hunde flitzen über die alten Teppiche, emsiges Personal hält den Haushalt tipptopp, und Mrs Vincent Astor telefoniert
ununterbrochen.

Pages précédentes et ci-dessus: Dans l'entrée comme dans tout l'appartement sont dispersés des meubles anciens chinois et de la porcelaine de Shanghaï où Brooke Astor a vécu avec ses parents avant 1910. On distingue au-dessus du canapé dans le grand salon un portrait de John Jacob Astor entouré de sa famille de 1850. Au-dessus du canapé, à gauche, des dessins et peintures du 18e siècle, réalisés entre autres par Tiepolo, Canaletto, Oudry et Boucher. Le tapis est un Axminster anglais datant de 1830 environ.
A droite: Les boiseries de la bibliothèque sont vernies en rouge sang-de-bœuf et rehaussées de baguettes en laiton. Le tapis ancien vient de Bessarabie.

Previous pages and above: In the foyer and scattered throughout the apartment are displays of antique Chinese furniture and porcelain from Shanghai, where, until 1910, Brooke Astor lived with her parents. Above the sofa in the large drawing room hangs a portrait of John Jacob Astor and his family, 1850. Left, above the sofa, are drawings and paintings by the 18th-century masters Tiepolo, Canaletto, Oudry and Boucher. The rug is English Axminster, circa 1830.
Right: the library paneling, lacquered in oxblood red. The antique carpet is from Bessarabia.

Vorhergehende Seiten und oben: Im Entrée und überall im Apartment verstreut steht altes chinesisches Mobiliar und Porzellan aus Shanghai, wo Brooke Astor mit ihren Eltern bis 1910 lebte. Über dem Sofa im großen Salon ein Porträt von John Jacob Astor und seiner Familie, 1850. Über dem Sofa links hängen Zeichnungen und Gemälde des 18. Jahrhunderts, unter anderen von Tiepolo, Canaletto, Oudry und Boucher. Der Teppich ist ein englischer Axminster von circa 1830.
Rechts: Die Täfelung in der Bibliothek ist ochsenblutrot lackiert und mit Messing abgesetzt. Der Teppich stammt aus Bessarabien.

Ci-dessus: la salle à manger: le couvert est dressé, l'argenterie anglaise côtoie le cristal de Bohème. Brooke Astor a trouvé les palmiers miniature au Caire et les a fait argenter plus tard. Les peintures murales sont de Jean Pillement, 18e siècle.

Pages suivantes de gauche, de gauche à droite et de haut en bas: le salon bleu: un cabinet anglais abrite une partie de la collection de chiens et de chats; «Deux chérubins» de François Boucher; une déesse ailée gréco-romaine, 200 avant J.-C.; au-dessus du sofa en chintz, un miroir Adam et une tapisserie flanquées d'acquarelles anglaises montrant des scènes orientales.

Pages suivantes de droite, de gauche à droite et de haut en bas: au-dessus de la cheminée en marbre de la bibliothèque: le tableau «Flags-Fith Avenue» réalisé par Childe Hassam en 1917 et en dessous, une pendule dorée Louis XVI avec des cochons en bronze d'Herbert Haseltine; dans l'entrée, «Chiens dansants et musiciens» de Giovanni Domenico Tiepolo, vers 1790; «Officiers en campagne» d'Ernest Meissonier, France, 1815; un dessin de Venise de James Holland, ainsi que «The Banyon Tree» d'Edward Lear sur une console française du 18e siècle, chien antique en marbre et coffre doré de Chine.

Above: the dining room. The table setting is English silver and Bohemian crystal. Brooke Astor found the miniature palm trees in Cairo and had them silver-plated. The wall-paintings are by Jean Pillement, 18th century.

Following pages left, clockwise from top left: the blue salon: An English cabinet displays a collection of antique and modern dogs and cats; "Two Cherubs" by François Boucher; a Greco-Roman winged goddess, 200 B.C.; above the chintz sofa hangs an Adam mirror and a petit point embroidery, flanked by 19th-century English watercolors of oriental scenes.

Following pages right, clockwise from top left: In the library, above the marble fireplace and gold Louis-XVI musical clock hangs Childe Hassam's "Flags – Fifth Avenue", 1917; in the foyer are "Dancing Dogs with Musicians" by Giovanni Domenico Tiepolo, circa 1790; the "Officers Riding to Battle" by Ernest Meissonier, France, 1815; above an 18th-century French console is a James Holland drawing of Venice and Edward Lear's "The Banyon Tree", the antique marble dog and gold chest are from China.

Oben: Blick in das Speisezimmer. Gedeckt ist mit englischem Silber und Kristall aus Böhmen. Die Miniaturpalmen fand Brooke Astor in Kairo und ließ sie später versilbern. Die Wandmalereien wurden von Jean Pillement im 18. Jahrhundert angefertigt.

Folgende Seiten links, im Uhrzeigersinn von links oben: der blaue Salon: in einem englischen Kabinettschränkchen ist ein Teil einer Sammlung von Hunde- und Katzenfiguren ausgestellt; »Zwei Putten« von François Boucher; der geflügelte Kopf einer antiken Göttin von ca. 200 v. Chr.; über dem Chintz-Sofa ein Adam-Spiegel und eine Petit-point-Stickerei, flankiert von englischen Aquarellen des 19. Jahrhunderts mit orientalischen Szenen.

Folgende Seiten rechts, im Uhrzeigersinn von links oben: in der Bibliothek »Flags – Fifth Avenue« von Childe Hassam von 1917, auf dem Marmorkamin eine vergoldete Louis-XVI-Spieluhr und zwei Bronzeschweine von Herbert Haseltine; im Entrée »Tanzende Hunde mit Musikanten« von Giovanni Domenico Tiepolo von ca. 1790; »Officiere reiten zur Schlacht« von dem französischen Maler Ernest Meissonier von 1815; die Zeichnungen »Ansicht von Venedig« von James Holland und »The Banyon Tree« von Edward Lear über einer französischen Konsole aus dem 18. Jahrhundert sowie ein Marmorhund und eine goldene Kiste aus China.

New York Interiors   Brooke Astor

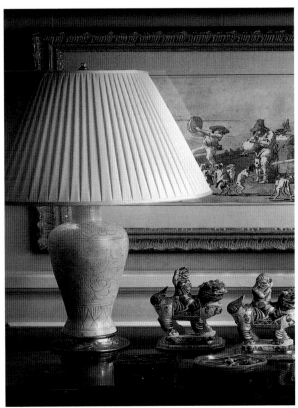

Issue d'une famille de braves artisans bernois, Susanne Bartsch, l'excentrique Reine de la Nuit, a fait la conquête de Manhattan du jour
au lendemain. Avec ses folles partys et ses shows, elle a lancé des
modes comme avec les Drag Queens et a fait accepter les hommes
habillés en femme. Devenue femme d'affaires, elle n'organise plus aujourd'hui que de grandes manifestations, des «Charity-Events» tels le
«Loveball» de New York ou la «Ballade de l'amour» de Paris. Elle
s'occupe de mode et a fondé une famille avec le beau culturiste David
Barton et leur fils Bailey. Il y a quinze ans, alors qu'elle était liée avec
le peintre Martine, elle a emménagé au Chelsea Hotel, West 23rd
Street, l'enclave légendaire des artistes. Mark Twain et Arthur Miller,
Janis Joplin et Sarah Bernhardt y ont vécu. C'est ici que Sid Vicious
des Sex Pistols a tué son amie à coups de couteau. Un jour, l'ami de
Bartsch est parti en lui laissant la suite au septième étage du Chelsea,
un appartement de quatre pièces à la fois extravagant et confortable.

Susanne Bartsch

Susanne Bartsch, a trademan's daughter from Berne, Switzerland,
transformed herself into Manhattan's Queen of the Night. Her wild
parties and shows kicked off many new styles, and made drag
socially acceptable. She now organizes big charity events such as
the New York "Loveball" and the Parisian "Ballade de l'amour."
Bartsch is also a fashion designer. She is married to the handsome
bodybuilder David Barton, and has a little son, Bailey. Fifteen years
ago she moved into the Chelsea Hotel, the legendary artists' enclave on West 23rd Street, with a friend, the painter Martine. Mark
Twain had lived here, as well as Arthur Miller, Janis Joplin and
Sarah Bernhardt. It was at the Chelsea that the Sex Pistols' Sid
Vicious stabbed his girlfriend to death. When Susanne Bartsch's
friend departed, he left her the four-room suite on the seventh floor
of the Chelsea, a chaotic but eminently comfortable apartment.

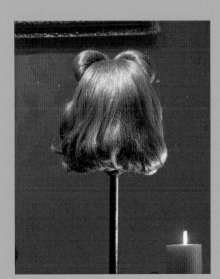

Sie stammt aus einer ganz normalen Berner Handwerkerfamilie und
hat Manhattan im Sturm erobert, Susanne Bartsch, die exzentrische
Königin der Nacht. Mit ihren wilden Parties und Shows hat sie Trends
gesetzt: So hat sie beispielsweise die Drag Queens, Männer in Frauen-
kleidern, salonfähig gemacht. Jetzt organisiert sie als Unternehmerin
nur noch »big« Charity-Events, wie den New Yorker »Loveball« und
die Pariser »Ballade de l'amour«. Außerdem entwirft sie Mode und
hat mit dem schönen Bodybuilder David Barton und Söhnchen
Bailey eine Familie gegründet. Vor 15 Jahren war sie als Freundin des
Malers Martine ins Chelsea Hotel gezogen, eine legendäre Künstler-
Enklave in der West 23rd Street. Vor ihr hatten dort schon Mark
Twain und Arthur Miller, Janis Joplin und Sarah Bernhardt gelebt.
Hier hatte auch Sid Vicious von den Sex Pistols seine Freundin ersto-
chen. Bartschs Gefährte setzte sich eines Tages ab und hinterließ ihr
die Vier-Zimmer-Suite im siebten Stock des Chelsea Hotels, eine
Wohnung ebenso skurril wie urgemütlich.

Pages précédentes et page de droite: *Dans le couloir de la suite de quatre pièces au Chelsea Hotel resplendit un cadeau d'anniversaire particulièrement pénétrant: le peintre Martine, ancien partenaire de la Party-Queen new-yorkaise Susanne Bartsch, a immortalisé son originale compagne dans une pose excitante. La photo de détail de la page précédente montre une sculpture capillaire – l'une des nombreuses perruques de Susanne Bartsch.*
Ci-dessus: *dans la chambre rouge en laque de Chine de Susanne Bartsch et de son mari, le culturiste dandy David Barton, un grand lit chinois au baldaquin en bois sculpté et recouvert de coussins brodés de fils d'or. La déesse indienne et le tableau du Christ, tout comme le miroir et le chandelier, viennent du marché aux puces.*

Previous pages and facing page: *The hall decor of the four-room Chelsea Hotel suite is an eye-catching birthday present from Martine, painter and ex-boyfriend of New York party queen Susanne Bartsch. He immortalized his unconventional wife in exciting poses. The detail photo on the previous page shows hair sculpture, one of Susanne Bartsch's many wigs.*
Above: *Susanne Bartsch and her husband, fitness dandy David Barton, have done their bedroom walls in red Chinese lacquer. Their spacious Chinese bed, decked with gold-embroidered pillows, has a finely carved wooden canopy. An Indian goddess, the painting of Christ, the mirror, and candle holders are fleamarket discoveries.*

Vorhergehende Seiten und rechte Seite: *Im Flur der Vier-Zimmer-Suite im Chelsea Hotel prangt ein schrilles Geburtstagsgeschenk: Martine, Kunstmaler und Ex-Freund der Party-Queen Susanne Bartsch, verewigte seine originelle Frau in aufregenden Posen. Das Detailfoto auf der vorhergehenden Seite zeigt eine Haar-Skulptur – eine von Susanne Bartschs vielen Perücken.*
Oben: *Im chinalackroten Schlafzimmer von Susanne Bartsch und ihrem Mann, Fitness-Dandy David Barton, steht ein großes chinesisches Bett mit kunstvoll geschnitztem Holzbaldachin und goldbestickten Kissen. Die indische Göttin und das Jesusbild stammen vom Flohmarkt, ebenso Spiegel und Kerzenständer.*

Ci-dessus à gauche: dans les années 70, des boules scintillantes dans une discothèque new-yorkaise, aujourd'hui dans la salle de bains des Bartsch une mosaïque réalisée par l'artiste new-yorkais Joey Horatio. Rideau de douche à la Alfred Hitchcock.

Ci-dessus à droite: La chambre d'enfant est pour Bailey, leur fils de deux ans. Restauré avec amour, le lit-cage a été offert par la famille de Berne. Susanne Bartsch, sa mère, sa grand-mère et son arrière-grand-mère y ont déjà dormi. La peinture murale est de Joey Horatio.

Page de droite: Joey Horatio a également décoré le salon rose aux ornements bleu ciel. Les fauteuils proviennent de ventes de l'Armée du Salut, les couvertures devant les protéger des chats. Susanne Bartsch a décoré elle-même le revêtement de la cheminée avec des entrelacs en fibre de verre. Sur la cheminée, un portrait en pied orné de médailles représentant son époux Barton dans toute sa splendeur et photographié par Francesco Scavullo.

Upper left: New York artist Joey Horatio did the mosaic design in the Bartsch bathroom with glittering tiles from a mirrored disco globe. The shower curtain brings Alfred Hitchcock's movies to mind.

Upper right: bedroom for two-year-old Bailey. His crib is a carefully restored present from the family in Berne. Susanne Bartsch slept in it, as did her mother, grandmother and great-grandmother before her. The wall decor is by Joey Horatio.

Facing page: The pink salon with sky-blue ornaments on the ceiling is also a design by Joey Horatio. The fauteuils, from the Salvation Army, are covered to protect them from the cats. Susanne Bartsch embellished the fireplace with ornaments she made from fiberglass. On the mantel is a portrait photo by Francesco Scavullo showing husband Barton in his full glory, with his medals adorning the frame.

Oben links: in den 70er Jahren Glitzerkugeln in einer New Yorker Diskothek, heute ein Mosaik im Badezimmer von Susanne Bartsch, arrangiert von dem New Yorker Künstler Joey Horatio. Duschvorhang à la Alfred Hitchcock.

Oben rechts: das Kinderzimmer des zweijährigen Sohns Bailey. Das liebevoll restaurierte Gitterbettchen ist ein Geschenk der Familie aus Bern. In ihm schliefen schon Susanne Bartsch, ihre Mutter, Großmutter und Urgroßmutter. Die Zeichnungen an der Wand stammen von Joey Horatio.

Rechte Seite: Den rosa Salon mit himmelblauen Ornamenten an der Decke hat ebenfalls Joey Horatio gestaltet. Die Fauteuils stammen vom Ramschverkauf der Heilsarmee, die Decken sollen sie vor den Katzen schützen. Die Kaminverkleidung hat Susanne Bartsch selbst mit Schnörkeln aus Fiberglas versehen. Auf dem Sims ein mit Medaillen geschmücktes ganzfiguriges Porträt von Ehemann Barton in voller Schönheit, fotografiert von Francesco Scavullo.

Bill Blass est le grand seigneur des stylistes de mode américains. Agé d'un peu plus de 70 ans, il a vécu un demi-siècle dans le monde trépidant de la mode au cœur de la légendaire 7th Avenue et maintenant il commence à se lasser de New York. En fait, il préfère sa maison de campagne dans le Connecticut, où il mène une vie tranquille et rustique, à son élégant appartement sur la East River. Il se rend donc toutes les semaines à Manhattan pour deux ou trois jours et réside alors dans son gigantesque appartement de la Sutton Place, où une grande partie de ses collections les plus diverses a pu trouver une place. Soldat pendant la Seconde Guerre mondiale, Blass est spécialiste des objets militaires de valeur et grand admirateur de l'art militaire – et de Napoléon. Partout, on voit s'affronter des guerriers et des soldats, des généraux et des capitaines: romains, grecs, anglais, français, de l'Antiquité à la Première Guerre mondiale. Par comparaison ses dessins et ses modèles d'escaliers, principalement du 19e siècle, semblent plutôt inoffensifs.

Bill Blass

Bill Blass is the *grand seigneur* of American fashion designers. Now in his early 70s, after fifty years in the tough fashion business on legendary 7th Avenue, he is beginning to get a little weary of New York. He would rather be in his quiet country home in rural Connecticut than in his elegant apartment on the East River. So he commutes only two or three times a week to Manhattan, where his enormous apartment, in a prime location on Sutton Place, harbors a large part of his varied collections. Bill Blass served in the army in World War II. He is an expert on top quality military paraphernalia and a great admirer of historical military art – and of Napoleon. The rooms swarm with warriors and soldiers, generals and strategists: Roman, Greek, British, French, from antiquity to the First World War. By comparison, his drawings and his model staircases, mainly from the 19th century, seem positively benign.

Bill Blass ist der Grandseigneur der amerikanischen Modedesigner. Mittlerweile ist er Anfang 70 und nach 50 Jahren im hektischen Mode-Business im Herzen der legendären 7th Avenue ein bißchen New-York-müde. Eigentlich zieht er das rustikal-ruhige Leben in seinem Landhaus in Connecticut seiner eleganten Stadtwohnung am East River vor. Deshalb fährt er jede Woche nur für zwei, drei Tage nach Manhattan hinein. Dort wohnt er in einem gigantischen Apartment in bester Lage am Sutton Place, in dem ein Großteil seiner unterschiedlichen Sammlungen Platz findet. Blass, der selbst Soldat im Zweiten Weltkrieg war, ist Spezialist für Militaria allererster Qualität sowie ein großer Bewunderer historischer Kriegskunst – und außerdem von Napoleon. Überall prallen sie in der Wohnung aufeinander: römische, griechische, englische und französische Krieger und Soldaten, Generäle und Feldherren von der Antike bis zum Ersten Weltkrieg. Vergleichsweise harmlos sind dagegen seine Zeichnungen und seine Sammlung von Modelltreppen, die hauptsächlich aus dem 19. Jahrhundert stammen.

Ci-dessus: vue sur les livres depuis le lit. Au milieu, une table de bibliothèque, de style Edouard. Dessus, quelques exemplaires de sa collection de modèles d'escaliers et un bronze de la colonne Vendôme érigée à la gloire de Napoléon. A droite, une statue équestre du jeune Napoléon, dans la bibliothèque Regency, des casques grecs du 6e siècle avant J.-C. La collection d'armes en trompe-l'œil est de Biltius et mesure 3 m de long.

Page de droite, de gauche à droite et de haut en bas: C'est dans la bibliothèque que l'on découvre les différentes passions de Bill Blass. Des bustes de guerriers côtoient des bronzes d'acrobates. Devant le miroir George Ier, une sculpture en bois des îles de Pâques. L'ordre règne dans le cabinet d'habillage: vestes et chemises sont rangées par couleur, chaise, Suède, 18e siècle, tableaux, Espagne, 17e siècle; des athlètes de bronze se prosternent devant des chaussures de faiseur.

Double page suivante: vue sur un petit parc et la East River. La chambre fait aussi office de bibliothèque et de salon. Le grand salon: encadrant la cheminée, deux méridiennes et deux bustes romains. Au-dessus de la cheminée, le dessin d'un vaisseau de guerre français. Au-dessus de la table de bibliothèque italienne, 19e siècle, quatre médaillons, Italie, 18e siècle.

Above: a view from the bed over to the books. In the center is an English Edwardian library table with pieces from Blass' stairs collection and a bronze miniature representing the column on Place Vendôme in Paris commemorating Napoleon's victories. On the right, a statue of the young Napoleon on horseback, on the Regency shelf Greek helmets from the 6th century B.C. The almost 3 m long trompe l'œil of a collection of arms is by Biltius.

Facing page, clockwise from top left: The library is where Bill Blass' collections mingle: busts of military men and bronzes of acrobats; a George I mirror reflects a wooden sculpture from the Easter Islands. Everything in the dressing room is in perfect order: jackets and shirts are arranged according to color, the chair is from 18th-century Swe-

den, the painting from 17th-century Spain; bronzes athletes bow to custom-fitted shoes.

Following pages: This is the view from the apartment over a small park and the East River. The fashion designer's bedroom doubles as library and drawing room. The fireplace is flanked by two Regency daybeds and by two Roman busts. Above the fireplace is a drawing of a French warship, and between the windows on the right, four medallions from 18th-century Italy.

Oben: Blick vom Bett auf die Bücher. In der Mitte ein englischer Edwardian Bibliothekstisch. Darauf einige Exemplare der Modelltreppen-Sammlung und eine Bronzekopie der Säule, die auf der Pariser Place Vendôme an den siegreichen Feldherrn Napoleon erinnert. Rechts eine Reiterstatue des jungen Napoleon, im Regency-Regal griechische Helme aus dem 6. Jahrhundert v. Chr. Das Trompe-l'œil einer Waffensammlung stammt von Biltius und mißt 3 m.

Rechte Seite, im Uhrzeigersinn von links oben: In der Bibliothek treffen die Passionen von Bill Blass aufeinander: Büsten von Soldaten stehen neben Bronzen von Akrobaten; vor dem George-I-Spiegel eine Holzskulptur von der Osterinsel. Penible Ordnung herrscht im Ankleidezimmer: Jackets und Hemden nach Farbe sortiert, Stuhl, Schweden, 18. Jahrhundert, Gemälde, Spanien, 17. Jahrhundert; bronzene Athleten verbeugen sich vor Maßschuhen.

Folgende Doppelseite: Blick aus dem Apartment hinunter auf den East River. Das Schlafzimmer ist gleichzeitig Bibliothek und Salon. Der Kamin wird flankiert von zwei Regency-Récamieren und zwei römischen Büsten. Über dem Kamin die Zeichnung eines französischen Schlachtschiffes. Rechts zwischen den Fenstern vier italienische Medaillons aus dem 18. Jahrhundert.

Pour l'architecte argentin Gustavo Bonevardi, chaque séjour dans son studio de West-Village représente un voyage sentimental dans son enfance. Son père, le peintre et sculpteur Marcelo Bonevardi, y a vécu du milieu des années 60 jusqu'à sa mort en 1994. Enfant, Gustavo venait déjà de Buenos Aires pour lui rendre visite, restant souvent des semaines entières. Il jouait sur le sol tandis que son père travaillait. Aucun décorateur n'a jamais mis les pieds dans ces lieux dont l'atmosphère créative provient tout simplement du fait qu'on y vit et y travaille. Aujourd'hui, Gustavo Bonevardi se sert de l'atelier paternel pour ses propres activités: le matériel du père et celui du fils se complètent au mieux. En fait, le fils qui travaille et enseigne à Buenos Aires n'est devenu designer qu'ici, à New York. Pour Gustavo Bonevardi, l'atelier de son père est une véritable mine d'or. Il y a ajouté quelques objets design des années 40 et des prototypes de ses propres créations de meubles, mais cela uniquement pour rendre un peu confortable le studio peu meublé du père.

Gustavo Bonevardi

Every time Argentine architect Gustavo Bonevardi enters his West Village studio, he feels he is taking a sentimental journey back into his childhood. His father, the artist Marcelo Bonevardi, lived there from the mid-60s until his death in 1994. Even as a small child, Gustavo used to come from Buenos Aires to visit, and while the father worked, the son played on the floor. Father and son never employed an interior designer. The highly creative atmosphere in the studio simply grew out of their lives and work, and their painting tools and implements complement each other perfectly. Bonevardi works and teaches in Buenos Aires, but it was in New York where his career really began. Every detail of the studio harbors fond memories of his father. It was only to make the ascetic space a bit more comfortable that Bonevardi added a few designer pieces from the 40s and some prototypes of his own design.

Jeder Aufenthalt des argentinischen Architekten Gustavo Bonevardi in seinem West-Village-Studio ist eine sentimentale Reise in die Kindheit. Sein Vater, der Maler und Bildhauer Marcelo Bonevardi, lebte hier seit Mitte der 60er Jahre bis zu seinem Tod 1994. Schon als kleiner Junge kam Gustavo oft für mehrere Wochen aus Buenos Aires zu Besuch und spielte auf dem Boden, während sein Vater arbeitete. Kein Innenarchitekt wurde jemals hierher bemüht. Die überaus kreative Atmosphäre ist einfach durch Leben und Arbeiten entstanden. Heute benutzt Gustavo Bonevardi das väterliche Atelier als seine eigene Werkstatt – Arbeitsmaterialien von Vater und Sohn ergänzen sich aufs beste. Tatsächlich hat der Sohn, der in Buenos Aires arbeitet und lehrt, erst hier in New York auch mit Designentwürfen begonnen. Für Gustavo Bonevardi ist jedes Detail in seines Vaters Atelier eine wertvolle Fundgrube. Um dem vom Vater sehr karg möblierten Studio ein wenig Bequemlichkeit zu verleihen, fügte Gustavo einige Designstücke aus den 40er Jahren und Prototypen seiner eigenen Möbelentwürfe hinzu.

Pages précédentes: *Gustavo a à peine modifié le studio de son père, l'artiste argentin Marcelo Bonevardi, mort en 1994. Seuls les deux fauteuils «The sphere in a cube» (Le monde dans un cube) sont une création personnelle. Au milieu de la pièce, une sculpture en grès et en acier de Marcelo Bonevardi, réalisée en 1986, sur le chevalet son tableau «Convent Windows» de 1990. La photo de détail montre partout des souvenirs du père: au mur à droite, une grande spatule qu'utilisait Marcelo Bonevardi pour travailler; devant, des balustrades et une suspension de camion qu'il avait trouvées dans la rue.*

Previous pages: *When his father, Argentinian artist Marcelo Bonevardi, died in 1994, Gustavo decided to preserve his studio largely as he left it. Only the two "The sphere in a cube" chairs are the architect and designer's own creations. In the center stands a sandstone and steel sculpture by Marcelo Bonevardi, 1986, on the easel his picture "Convent Windows", 1990. The detail photo shows memories of his father everywhere: at right, on the wall, is a broad spatula which Marcelo Bonevardi used for his work, in the foreground, balustrades and truck springs he found on the street.*

Vorhergehende Seiten: *Das Studio des 1994 verstorbenen argentinischen Künstlers Marcelo Bonevardi hat sein Sohn Gustavo kaum verändert. Nur die beiden »The sphere in a cube«-Sessel (Welt im Würfel) sind eigene Entwürfe. In der Mitte des Raumes eine Skulptur von Marcelo Bonevardi aus Sandstein und Stahl von 1986, auf der Staffelei sein Bild »Convent Windows« von 1990. Auf dem Detailfoto sieht man überall Erinnerungen an den Vater: an der Wand rechts ein breiter Spachtel, mit dem Marcelo Bonevardi arbeitete, vorne Baluster und eine Lastwagenfeder, die er auf der Straße gefunden hatte.*

New York Interiors   Gustavo Bonevardi

Page de gauche, en haut: dans la salle de séjour, des œuvres de
Marcelo Bonevardi. A partir de la gauche: «Project for a Magic Box»,
1983, «Shadow», 1990, derrière la table «Phases of the Moon», 1990.
Page de gauche, en bas: vue de la cuisine.
A droite: dans le studio, l'attirail du peintre.
Ci-dessous: C'est Le Corbusier qui a créé en 1929 ce sofa luxueux
intitulé «Grand Confort». Devant, une chaise LCW de Charles et Ray
Eames, 1946. Des œuvres de Marcelo Bonevardi, entre autres à
gauche «Trapped Angel», 1978, et au milieu «False Door», 1990.
Sur l'étagère à droite, figurines et objets précolombiens.

Facing page above: The living area features works by Marcelo
Bonevardi. From left to right: "Project for a Magic Box", 1983,
"Shadow", 1990, and behind the dining-room table "Phases of
the Moon", 1990.
Facing page below: a view into the kitchen.
Right: in the studio, tools of the artist's trade.
Below: The luxurious "Grand-Comfort" sofa is a design by Le Corbusier, 1929. In front an LCW-chair by Charles and Ray Eames. The
art is by Marcelo Bonevardi, including left "Trapped Angel", 1978,
and center "False Door", 1990. The shelves to the right contain a
collection of pre-Columbian figures and artifacts.

Linke Seite oben: im Wohnbereich Werke von Marcelo Bonevardi.
Von links: »Project for a Magic Box« von 1983, »Shadow« von 1990,
hinter dem Eßtisch »Phases of the Moon« von 1990.
Linke Seite unten: Blick in die Küche.
Rechts: das Handwerkszeug des Künstlers im Atelier.
Unten: Das luxuriöse »Grand-Comfort«-Sofa entwarf Le Corbusier
1929. Vorne ein LCW-Stuhl von Charles und Ray Eames. Kunst von
Marcelo Bonevardi, u.a. links »Trapped Angel« von 1978 und »False
Door« von 1990 (Mitte). Im Regal rechts präkolumbianische Figuren
und Artefakte.

Steve Bonge est le chef de la légendaire et puissante communauté des Hells Angels de la ville de New York, où il est connu comme le loup blanc. Devant la maison de briques qu'il habite et qui est en même temps le point de rencontre de ses amis et compagnons, sont toujours garées de nombreuses Harley Davidson reluisantes. Le bâtiment d'ardoises goudronné est situé Downtown, à East Village, dans la 2nd Street, entre la 1st et la 2nd Avenue, c'est l'un de ces immeubles de rapport caractéristiques, construits au tournant du siècle pour loger les travailleurs, et qui marquent de leur sceau ce quartier de New York. Les pièces sont petites et basses, mais si on accorde ici peu d'importance au confort, l'ambiance compte beaucoup. L'appartement de Bonge est un musée du grotesque, tous les murs sont remplis de souvenirs de ses passions très variées. On y voit aussi bien des jantes que des images Fantasy, des ustensiles de trappeur que des couvercles de cercueil.

Steve Bonge

Steve Bonge is head of the New York City chapter of the legendary motorcycle club Hells Angels, and as such, his name is a byword not only to initiates. Rows of gleaming Harley Davidsons stand outside the building he lives in, a favorite meeting point for friends and acquaintances. The blackened brick structure, located Downtown, in the East Village, on 2nd Street between 1st and 2nd Avenue, is one of the tenements typical of his part of town, built around the turn of the century for working people. The rooms are accordingly small and low-ceilinged, but what they may lack in comfort is more than made up for by their atmosphere. Bonge's apartment is a bizarre museum, every wall of it covered with memorabilia of his various interests – from hub caps to fantasy pictures, from trapper's equipment to coffin lids.

Steve Bonge ist Chef der legendären und mächtigen Motorrad-Gemeinde, der Hells Angels von New York City, über die Szene hinaus bekannt wie ein bunter Hund. Und so stehen vor dem Backsteinhaus, in dem er wohnt und das gleichzeitig Meeting-Point für Freunde und Gefährten ist, stets etliche blankpolierte Harley Davidsons. Das schwarz geteerte Ziegelsteingebäude liegt Downtown, im East Village, in der 2nd Street zwischen 1st und 2nd Avenue, und ist eines dieser typischen, diesen Teil New Yorks prägenden, Tenement Buildings, um die Jahrhundertwende als Mietshaus für Arbeiter erbaut. Entsprechend klein und niedrig sind die Zimmer, auf Komfort wird hier wenig Wert gelegt, um so mehr auf Atmosphäre. Sein Apartment ist ein skurriles Museum, alle Wände sind dicht an dicht behängt mit Memorabila seiner unterschiedlichen Leidenschaften. Von Radkappen bis Fantasy-Kult-Bildern, von Trapper-Utensilien bis Sargdeckeln.

Double page précédente: Le séjour est dominé par une vieille pompe à essence Texaco et un cercueil noir éclairé au néon. Des rideaux de tulle noir laissent filtrer une lumière diffuse.
Page de gauche: la volumineuse collection d'enjoliveurs de Steve Bonge.
En haut: la petite chambre à coucher: motifs sombres sur murs blancs, des illustrations Fantasy sataniques, un couvercle de cercueil, une poupée vaudou sur le lit étroit. Sur le tout veille un superbe ancien équipement de trappeur.
A droite: dans le réfrigérateur, une nature morte à l'Agneau mystique.

Previous pages: The living room is dominated by a vintage Texaco gas pump and a neon-illuminated black coffin, gleaming in the diffuse light that falls through black gauze curtains.
Facing page: Steve Bonge's extensive collection of hub caps.
Above: the bedroom, long and narrow, features dark motifs on white walls, satanic fantasy illustrations, a coffin lid, and a voodoo doll at the head of the bed. Watching over it all is a beautiful set of antique trapper's clothing and equipment.
Right: a refrigerator still life with sacrificial lamb.

Vorhergehende Doppelseite: Im Wohnraum dominieren eine alte Texaco-Zapfsäule und ein neon-illuminierter schwarzer Sarg. Schwarze Gazevorhänge spenden diffuses Licht.
Linke Seite: die umfangreiche Radkappensammlung von Steve Bonge.
Oben: das schmale Schlafzimmer: dunkle Motive auf weißen Wänden, satanische Fantasy-Illustrationen, ein Sargdeckel, auf dem schmalen Bett eine Voodoo-Puppe. Über all dem wacht eine prachtvolle alte Trapper-Ausrüstung.
Rechts: im Kühlschrank ein Stilleben mit Opferlamm.

Grand seigneur et créateur de mode, Oleg Cassini vit dans une maison comptant parmi les curiosités de New York. Construite au 17e siècle à Amsterdam par de riches bourgeois hollandais, elle fut démolie en 1845, transportée par bateau dans le Nouveau Monde et reconstruite, pierre par pierre, dans la Upper West Side de Manhattan pour servir de résidence privée aux négociants new-yorkais Wells. Armures et armes, drapeaux et blasons sont la passion de Cassini. Tout au long de sa vie aventureuse, il a rassemblé des antiquités et des tableaux provenant surtout d'Italie, de France, d'Espagne et d'Allemagne. Son père, de nationalité russe, était ambassadeur du Tsar à Washington, sa mère, une duchesse italienne. Cassini, lui, est né à Paris et a consacré sa vie aux plus belles femmes du monde. Il fut l'ami de Grace Kelly avant qu'elle ne rencontre le prince Rainier de Monaco, il a habillé les stars d'Hollywood dont Natalie Wood et Marilyn Monroe, puis plus tard Jacqueline Kennedy quand celle-ci devint la femme du Président.

Oleg Cassini

Oleg Cassini, fashion czar and leading designer, lives in a New York landmark. The house was built by wealthy Dutch burghers in Amsterdam in the 17th century. In 1845 it was dismantled and shipped to the New World. On Manhattan's Upper West Side, New York merchants reconstructed the house, making it their private home. Armor and weapons, flags and heraldic symbols are Cassini's passion. In the course of his life he has collected antiques and paintings of the 15th and 16th centuries. His father was the Czar's Russian Ambassador in Washington, his mother an Italian duchess. Cassini was born in Paris and has dedicated his life to the world's most beautiful women. He was Grace Kelly's companion before she met Prince Rainier of Monaco. The biggest Hollywood stars, such as Natalie Wood and Marilyn Monroe, wore his designs. Later, Oleg Cassini was Jacqueline Kennedy's personal designer.

Oleg Cassini, Grandseigneur und Modeschöpfer, lebt in einer New Yorker Sehenswürdigkeit. Sein Haus wurde im 17. Jahrhundert in Amsterdam von Patriziern erbaut, 1845 dort abgetragen, in die Neue Welt verschifft und als Privathaus für die New Yorker Kaufleute Wells in der Upper West Side von Manhattan Stein für Stein wiederaufgebaut. Betritt man die pompöse Wohnhalle, so fühlt man sich eher wie in einem mittelalterlichen Rittersaal als im Salon eines Gentleman. Rüstungen und Waffen, Flaggen und Wappen sind Cassinis Leidenschaft. Im Laufe seines abenteuerlichen Lebens hat er Antiquitäten und Gemälde aus dem 15. und 16. Jahrhundert zusammengetragen, vorwiegend aus Italien, Frankreich, Spanien und Deutschland. Sein Vater war Botschafter des Zaren in Washington, seine Mutter eine italienische Herzogin. Cassini selbst ist in Paris geboren und hat sein Leben den schönsten Frauen der Welt gewidmet. Er war der Gefährte von Grace Kelly, bevor sie Fürst Rainier von Monaco traf, er kleidete Hollywoodstars wie Natalie Wood und Marilyn Monroe, später auch Jacqueline Kennedy, als sie First Lady war.

Ci-dessus: un mélange de styles extravagant dans la salle de séjour: canapés anglais en cuir, peaux de zèbre d'Afrique, tableaux de la Renaissance italienne, une énorme cheminée en stuc blanc supportant un triptyque néerlandais peint vers 1500.
Double page suivante: A mi-chemin entre la salle d'armes et la nef d'église, la pièce principale de la maison est bien la salle de séjour, haute de 7 m.

Above: The living area displays a mix of extravagant styles: leather sofas from England, zebra skins from Africa, paintings from the Italian Renaissance, an oversized fireplace of white stucco. Above the fireplace is a triptych, circa 1500, from the Netherlands.
Following pages: The main room of the home with its 7 m high ceiling is a blend of manorial hall and church nave.

Oben: in der Wohnhalle eine extravagante Stilmischung: englische Ledersofas, Zebrafelle aus Afrika, Gemälde der italienischen Renaissance, ein gewaltiger Kamin aus weißem Stuck, darüber ein niederländisches Triptychon, um 1500.
Folgende Doppelseite: Der Hauptraum des Hauses, die 7 m hohe Wohnhalle, ist halb Rittersaal, halb Kirchenschiff.

Né à Trieste à l'époque où la ville appartenait encore à l'Empire aus-tro-hongrois, Leo Castelli est sans aucun doute le plus important mar-chand d'art du monde, même s'il s'en défend. Il affirme aussi qu'il n'est en aucun cas un collectionneur d'œuvres d'art. Néanmoins, dans son appartement de la Fifth Avenue – situé dans une maison bâtie en 1940, l'année de son arrivée à New York – il vit parmi les œuvres des artistes qu'il a découverts et encouragés. Et il fait du négoce. Dans le salon, la chambre, le couloir, la salle de bains, on trouve des œuvres de Jasper Johns, Roy Lichtenstein, Frank Stella, Frank Gehry, Charles et Ray Eames, Andy Warhol, Isamu Noguchi, Robert Rauschenberg, Jackson Pollock, Willem de Kooning, Franz Kline, Yves Klein, Cy Twombly, Claes Oldenburg, Ellsworth Kelly, Bruce Nauman, Richard Serra, James Rosenquist, pour n'en citer que quelques-uns. En ce moment pourtant, le grand charmeur affectionne plus que tout une carte placée sur le rebord de la cheminée: elle lui a été envoyée par Sharon Stone qui aimerait bien le revoir.

Leo Castelli

Leo Castelli was born in Trieste when it was still part of the Austro-Hungarian Empire. He is the most significant art dealer in the world, a description that he downplays, adding that he definitely is not a collector. His Fifth Avenue apartment was built in 1940, the year he arrived in New York. It is filled with works of art by artists he discovered and promoted, and whose works he sells. Displayed in the drawing room, the bedroom, the corridor, and the bathroom are works by artists such as Jasper Johns, Roy Lichtenstein, Frank Stella, Andy Warhol, Robert Rauschenberg, Jackson Pollock, Willem de Kooning, Franz Kline, Yves Klein, Cy Twombly, Claes Oldenburg, Ellsworth Kelly, Bruce Nauman, Richard Serra, James Rosenquist, just to name a few. Presently, of course, the old charmer's most precious item is a greeting from Sharon Stone, who would like to see him again.

Leo Castelli, in Triest geboren, als es noch zur österreichisch-ungari-schen k. u. k.-Monarchie gehörte, ist zweifellos der bedeutendste Kunsthändler der Welt, was er gern herunterspielt. Er sei auch keines-wegs Kunstsammler, sagt er. Dennoch lebt er in seinem Fifth-Avenue-Apartment – in einem Haus, das 1940 gebaut wurde, dem Jahr, in dem er nach New York kam – inmitten der Werke der Künstler, die er entdeckt und gefördert hat. Im Salon, im Schlafzimmer, im Flur, im Bad befinden sich Werke von Jasper Johns, Roy Lichtenstein, Frank Stella, Frank Gehry, Charles und Ray Eames, Andy Warhol, Isamu Noguchi, Robert Rauschenberg, Jackson Pollock, Willem de Kooning, Franz Kline, Yves Klein, Cy Twombly, Claes Oldenburg, Ellsworth Kelly, Bruce Nauman, Richard Serra, James Rosenquist – um nur ein paar zu nennen. Zur Zeit ist dem großen Charmeur allerdings eine Karte auf dem Kaminsims am wertvollsten: ein Gruß von Sharon Stone, die ihn gern wiedersehen möchte.

Page de gauche: Castelli avec la boîte Brillo d'Andy Warhol, qui, recouverte de plexiglas, sert aujourd'hui de table basse dans la salle de
séjour de son appartement de la Fifth Avenue. «Cup of coffee» de
Roy Lichtenstein, 1962, et sur la table sa «Ceramic Sculpture».
Ci-dessus: On peut rencontrer Leo Castelli tous les jours de onze
heures du matin à sept heures du soir – sauf le dimanche et à l'heure
des repas – dans sa Galerie à SoHo, 420 West Broadway. Ici, devant
«Interior» réalisé par Roy Lichtenstein en 1961 avec Yves Klein.

Facing page: Castelli with a Brillo Box by Andy Warhol, which is now
encased in plexiglass and serves as a side table in the living room of
his Fifth Avenue apartment. Roy Lichtenstein's "Cup of Coffee", 1962.
On the table is his "Ceramic Sculpture".
Above: From eleven to seven Leo Castelli is in his gallery in SoHo,
420 West Broadway. Behind him the wall-filling "Interior" by Roy
Lichtenstein and Yves Klein, 1961.

Linke Seite: Castelli mit der Brillo-Box von Andy Warhol, die heute –
in Plexiglas gesetzt – in seinem Fifth-Avenue-Apartment als Beistell-
tischchen im Wohnzimmer dient. Roy Lichtensteins »Cup of Coffee«
von 1962 und auf dem Tisch seine »Ceramic Sculpture«.
Oben: Täglich – außer sonntags und zur Mittagszeit – ist Leo Castelli
von elf Uhr morgens bis sieben Uhr abends in seiner Galerie in SoHo,
420 West Broadway anzutreffen. Hier steht er vor dem Gemälde
»Interior«, das Roy Lichtenstein mit Yves Klein 1961 schuf.

Au-dessus du lit de Castelli, «Dreams» d'Edward Ruscha, 1987. Pas sur la photo: sa collection de Léos — hommage au roi des animaux, cartes postales, affiches et jouets offerts au fil des ans par ses amis.

Above Castelli's bed is Edward Ruscha's "Dreams", 1987. Not in the picture: his collection of Leo king-of-the-animals memorabilia — postcards, posters, and toys given to him by his friends and admirers over the years.

Über Castellis Bett »Dreams« von Edward Ruscha von 1987. Nicht im Foto: seine Sammlung von Leo-Memorabilien, dem König der Tiere — Postkarten, Poster und Spielzeuge, die Freundinnen und Freunde ihm im Laufe der Jahrzehnte verehrt haben.

Dans la salle de séjour, au-dessus de la cheminée, le célèbre «Flag»
de Jasper Johns, réalisé en 1958 et représentant le drapeau américain
avec ses 48 étoiles pour les 48 Etats de l'époque (aujourd'hui 51).
Dans la cheminée, «Yellow Apple», un bronze peint en jaune de Roy
Lichtenstein, 1981. Petite table de Jean et Jacques Adnet. Le lampadaire en forme de serpent est d'Edgar Brandt, 1925, le tapis exécuté
aux Indes, de Frank Stella. Fauteuil Charles X. A droite, «Target with
Plaster Casts» de Jasper Johns, 1955.

In the living room above the fireplace is Jasper John's renowned
"Flag", 1958, still with 48 stars. In the fireplace, Roy Lichtenstein's
bronze sculpture "Yellow Apple" of 1981. The side table is by Jean and
Jacques Adnet, the snake lamp by Edgar Brandt, 1925. The carpet
was handmade in India to a Frank Stella design. The armchair is
from the Charles X period. On the right "Target with Plaster Casts"
by Jasper Johns, 1955.

Im Wohnraum über dem Kamin Jasper Johns berühmte »Flag« von
1958, die amerikanische Flagge mit 48 Sternen, die damals erst 48
der heute 51 Staaten repräsentierten. Im Kamin Roy Lichtensteins
»Yellow Apple« von 1981, eine gelb bemalte Bronze. Tischchen von
Jean und Jacques Adnet. Die Stehlampe in Form einer Schlange fer-
tigte Edgar Brandt 1925. In Indien geknüpfter Teppich von Frank
Stella. Armlehnstuhl aus der Zeit von Charles X. Rechts »Target with
Plaster Casts« von Jasper Johns von 1955.

Ci-dessus et détail: Comme à l'intérieur d'un coquillage, l'escalier relie le rez-de-chaussée au deuxième étage. Au pied de l'escalier, la lampe-poisson de Frank Gehry se tient en sentinelle.
Page de droite: On ne saurait imaginer plus grand contraste. Chiat a fait complètement vider la maison construite en 1902 dans le style Renaissance néerlandaise et fait installer à l'intérieur un loft ultramoderne. Au-dessus de la porte d'entrée, des têtes de chevaux en stuc; sous le faîte du toit, une tête de bouledogue.

Above and detail photo: The winding staircase leading from the first to the second floor calls to mind the inside of a snail shell. The fish lamp by Frank Gehry guards the foot of the stairs.
Facing page: No contrast can be greater than Chiat's home before and after remodeling. He extracted the contents of the entire house, built in Dutch Renaissance style in 1902, and installed an ultramodern loft inside. Above the entrance are bulldogs, under the ridge of the roof is a stucco horse head.

Oben und Detailfoto: Wie durch das Innere einer Muschel führt die Wendeltreppe vom Parterre bis hinauf in die zweite Etage. Am Fuß der Treppe wacht die Fischlampe von Frank Gehry.
Rechte Seite: Größer kann kein Kontrast sein: Chiat ließ das 1902 im niederländischen Renaissance-Stil erbaute Haus völlig entkernen und im Inneren einen ultramodernen Loft installieren. Über dem Eingang Pferdeköpfe aus Stuck, unter dem Dachfirst ein Bulldoggenkopf.

Jay Chiat, l'un des cerveaux les plus créatifs du monde de la publicité, est New-Yorkais à cent pour cent. Né dans le Bronx, il a grandi à Brooklyn et vit aujourd'hui à Midtown Manhattan. Afin d'avoir plus de place pour son importante collection d'art contemporain, Chiat a fait abattre les murs intérieurs de sa demeure, une ancienne maison de cocher construite en 1902, et a ainsi obtenu des pièces ayant la taille de salles d'exposition. Là, le directeur du Museum of Contemporary Art de New York vit maintenant entouré des meilleurs parmi les meilleurs: Joseph Beuys, Cy Twombly, Robert Rauschenberg, Jasper Johns et Frank Stella, et bien d'autres encore. «Une moitié de moi a besoin d'ordre et est fascinée par l'art minimaliste, l'autre moitié mène une vie assez chaotique», dit-il. Apparemment, la maison n'est pas conçue pour une famille. Car s'il est père de trois enfants adultes et grand-père-gâteau, il est redevenu, après deux divorces, un célibataire endurci.

Jay Chiat

Jay Chiat, a creative giant in the world of international advertising and Curator of the Museum of Contemporary Art, is a New Yorker through and through. He was born in the Bronx, grew up in Brooklyn and now lives in midtown Manhattan. To make room for his outstanding collection of contemporary art, he gutted a 1902 coach house and turned it into an expansive museum, which boasts the best of such as Joseph Beuys, Cy Twombly, Jasper Johns, and Frank Stella, to name a few. "One half of me needs perfect order and is fascinated with minimal art. The other half leads a pretty chaotic life," Chiat says. His home does not seem to be family-oriented. Though the father of three grown children who adores his grandchildren, Chiat enjoys being a bachelor again.

Jay Chiat, einer der kreativsten Köpfe der internationalen Werbeszene, ist ein waschechter New Yorker. In der Bronx geboren und in Brooklyn aufgewachsen lebt er heute in Midtown Manhattan. Um Platz für seine bedeutende Sammlung zeitgenössischer Kunst zu schaffen, ließ er das ehemalige Kutscherhaus von 1902 völlig entkernen und gewann so Räume mit Dimensionen einer Kunsthalle. Hier lebt der Kurator des New Yorker Museum of Contemporary Art umgeben von den Besten der Besten, von Joseph Beuys, Cy Twombly, Robert Rauschenberg, Jasper Johns, Frank Stella und vielen anderen. »Meine eine Hälfte braucht Ordnung und ist fasziniert von minimalistischer Kunst, meine andere führt ein ziemlich chaotisches Leben«, sagt er. Das Haus ist ganz offensichtlich nicht familiengerecht. Chiat ist zwar Vater von drei erwachsenen Kindern und begeisterter Großvater, aber nach zwei Scheidungen wieder überzeugter Junggeselle.

Attention, œuvre d'art: le célèbre «South American Circle» de Bruce Nauman, 1981, un anneau en acier massif d'un diamètre de près de 5 m, est suspendu à hauteur de la tête dans l'entrée de la maison de Jay Chiat.

Danger! Art! In the entrance to Jay Chiat's home, suspended slightly above head height, is the well-known "South American Circle" by Bruce Nauman, 1981, a solid steel ring almost 5 m in diameter.

Vorsicht Kunst: Im Eingang von Jay Chiats Haus schwebt knapp über Kopfhöhe der berühmte »South American Circle« von Bruce Nauman von 1981, ein massiver Stahlring mit einem Durchmesser von fast 5 m.

A droite: la cuisine, une froide atmosphère d'aluminium.
Ci-dessous: la salle de séjour. Au-dessus de la cheminée, une toile de
Robert Therrien, 1986, ayant la forme d'ailes déployées; à gauche, les
«White Constellations» monochromes d'Imi Knoebel, 1983, flottent
au-dessus des «Aluminium Boxes» de Donald Judd, 1986. Les fauteuils sont une copie réalisée par Ecart International, Paris du «Siège
transat», créé en 1927 par Eileen Gray pour une villa à Roquebrune
sur la côte d'Azur. Canapés de Mario Bellini.

Right: Cool aluminum dominates the kitchen.
Below: the living room. Above the fireplace a canvas by Robert
Therrien, 1986, evoking a great bird in flight. Suspended on the left,
above Donald Judd's "Aluminium Boxes", 1986, are Imi Knoebel's
monochrome "White Constellations", 1983. The armchairs are copies
of "Siège transat", which Eileen Gray designed in 1927 for a villa in
Roquebrune on the Côte D'Azur. The sofas are by Mario Bellini.

Rechts: In der Küche dominiert kühles Aluminium.
Unten: der Wohnraum. Über dem Kamin ein Gemälde von Robert
Therrien von 1986 mit stilisierten Vogelflügeln, links schweben Imi
Knoebels monochrome »White Constellations« von 1983 über den
»Aluminium Boxes« von Donald Judd. Die Sessel sind eine Nach-
bildung des »Siège transat«, den Eileen Gray 1927 für eine Villa in
Roquebrune an der Côte d'Azur entwarf. Sofas von Mario Bellini.

En tant que vice-président et creative director de la chaîne de magasins de luxe Barney's, Simon Doonan est responsable entre autres des décorations excentriques des magasins. Son appartement, en bas de la Fifth Avenue, est si petit qu'il pourrait entrer tout entier dans l'une des grandes vitrines Barney's de la 7th Avenue. Son aménagement est une véritable accumulation de curiosités et, comme le dit Doonan lui-même, il est tout ce que l'on veut sauf confortable. Le confort est pour lui un mot impossible, synonyme de mauvaise habitude. La controverse, à la limite la laideur, voilà ce qui l'attire davantage. Il franchit allègrement les barrières du kitsch, comme avec cette lampe des années 70 achetée sans doute au rayon des luminaires dans une grande surface à petits prix. De telles ruptures de style l'amusent énormément. Et lorsque sa mère lui proposa de broder des coussins pour ses chaises de jardin, entre parenthèses hautement inconfortables, il accepta avec joie. Bien entendu. Rien n'aurait pu être assez gentil et mignon pour ses coussins.

Simon Doonan

Simon Doonan is Vice-President and Creative Director of the high-class department-store chain Barney's. He is also responsible for the prestigious chain's eccentric decorations. His apartment on lower Fifth Avenue is so small that it would fit entire into one of Barney's 7th Avenue show windows. He agrees that the accumulation of curios makes his apartment less than comfortable. For Simon Doonan, cozy is a fourletter word. What he loves is the bizarre to ugly, including kitsch such as his 70s lamp with its five-and-dime store flavor. Grotesque items lacking in style give him great pleasure. He was obviously elated when his mother offered to crochet covers for the pillows on his extremely uncomfortable garden chairs. They couldn't be cutesy enough.

Als Vice President und Creative Director der Edel-Kaufhauskette Barney's ist Simon Doonan unter anderem für die exzentrischen Dekorationen verantwortlich. Sein Apartment an der unteren Fifth Avenue ist so klein, daß es komplett in eines der großen Schaufenster von Barney's an der 7th Avenue passen würde. Die Einrichtung ist eine wahre Akkumulation von Kuriositäten und – wie Doonan selbst sagt – alles andere als komfortabel. Gemütlichkeit ist für ihn ein Unwort und eine Unart. Kontrovers und beinahe häßlich – das interessiert ihn schon eher. Die Grenze zum Kitsch darf gern überschritten werden, wie z.B. bei der 70er-Jahre-Lampe, die vermutlich aus der Lampenabteilung eines Billigkaufhauses stammt. Solch groteske Stilbrüche machen ihm richtig Spaß. Und als ihm seine Mutter anbot, Kissenbezüge für seine äußerst unbequemen Gartenstühle zu stricken, war er selbstverständlich hocherfreut. Sie konnten ihm nicht niedlich genug sein.

Pages précédentes: *vue depuis la galerie sur l'excentrique salle de séjour de Simon Doonan. Le meuble blanc provient d'un marché aux puces de l'Armée du Salut. Le fauteuil ovoïde d'Arne Jacobsen, 1958, lui rappelle Emma Peel de la série télévisée «Chapeau melon et bottes de cuir». Le tapis rouge vif en tricot est une fabrication hors-série. Sur la photo de détail on voit les drôles de carafes à vin de Murano.*
Ci-dessus: *vue de la galerie-balcon.*
Page de droite: *De grosses veines en fragments de pare-brises colorés parcourent la section de tronc formant la table. Chaises Pedestal d'Eero Saarinen, 1957. Lampe des années 70, imitation écailles et gland doré.*

Previous pages: *view from the gallery down to Simon Doonan's eccentric living room. The white sideboard is from the Salvation Army thrift shop. The Egg Chair by Arne Jacobsen, 1958, reminds him of Diana Rigg's Emma Peel in the television series "The Avengers". The bright-red knitted carpet was custom-made. The detail photo shows amusing wine decanters from Murano near Venice, Italy.*
Above: *view towards the balcony-gallery.*
Facing page: *The tree-trunk top of the dining-room table is interlaced with thick veins of tinted glass from windshields. The pedestal chairs are by Eero Saarinen, 1957. The 70s lamp is made of imitation tortoise-shell with a simulated gold tassel.*

Vorhergehende Seiten: *Blick von der Galerie auf den exzentrischen Wohnraum von Simon Doonan. Das weiße Sideboard stammt von einem Flohmarkt der Heilsarmee. Der Egg-Sessel von Arne Jacobsen erinnert ihn an Emma Peel aus der Kult-Serie »Mit Schirm, Charme und Melone«. Der knallrote Strick-Teppich ist eine Sonderanfertigung. Auf dem Detailfoto sieht man witzige Wein-Karaffen aus Murano.*
Oben: *Blick auf die Balkongalerie.*
Rechte Seite: *Durch die baumstammförmige Platte des Eßtisches ziehen sich dicke Adern aus den Scherben getönter Windschutzscheiben. Tulip-Stühle von Eero Saarinen von 1957. 70er-Jahre-Lampe aus imitiertem Schildpatt und mit falscher Goldquaste.*

Avec ses épais murs en briques, ses larges passages voûtés, ses pavés usés et ses lourdes portes en métal brut, cette ancienne usine de Long Island City, située dans la partie nord-ouest du Queens, semble n'avoir jamais été remise à neuf. Mais ce n'est que la première impression. Tim et Dagny Du Val ont travaillé près de deux ans à la restauration de cette ancienne fonderie du 18e siècle, qui fut transformée plus tard en usine de crèmes glacées. Leur but était de donner à ce bâtiment sévère une atmosphère chaude et accueillante. Ils semblent y être parvenus. Malgré tout, bâtiments et arrière-cours ont retrouvé en grande partie leur état industriel primitif. Les Du Val ont conservé aussi bien les portes d'ascenseur en fer rouillé que les rigoles d'écoulement dans le sol. Les poutres de la grande chambre froide servent aujourd'hui de bar dans la cuisine. A côté de l'usine, les Du Val s'adonnent à l'horticulture. Il n'est donc pas étonnant que ce soient les plantes, et non les œuvres d'art, qui décorent leurs grandes pièces.

Tim and Dagny Du Val

Tim and Dagny Du Val's old factory building is in Long Island City, a part of New York directly across the East River from Manhattan. Its brick walls, wide-arched portals, worn paving stone floors, and heavy metal doors give the impression of having stood here unchanged for a century. Actually the Du Vals worked for almost two years restoring the former 18th-century foundry that later became an ice cream factory. In their friends' view, the factory now has an almost Italian Renaissance flavour. To a large extent, buildings and courtyards have been returned to their original industrial state. Rusted iron elevator doors were retained; wooden beams from the cooling chamber now serve as a kitchen counter. Next door, the Du Vals operate their landscape gardening firm. No wonder plants play the prime decorative role in their home.

Dicke Backsteinmauern, weite Torbögen, abgetretene Pflastersteinböden und schwere Türen aus rohem Metall lassen das alte Fabrikgebäude in Long Island City, im Nordwesten von Queens, nur auf den ersten Blick unberührt erscheinen. Tim und Dagny Du Val haben fast zwei Jahre an der Restaurierung der ehemaligen Gießerei aus dem 18. Jahrhundert gearbeitet – später befand sich hier eine Speiseeisfabrik. Ihr Ziel, dem kalten Gebäude eine warme und gemütliche Atmosphäre zu geben, scheint gelungen zu sein. Denn Freunde sagen, das Fabrikensemble verströme nach der Restaurierung einen Hauch von italienischer Renaissance. Trotzdem sind Gebäude und Hinterhöfe größenteils in den industriellen Urzustand zurückversetzt. Aufzugtüren aus verrostetem Eisen wurden ebenso erhalten wie Abflußrinnen im Boden. Holzbalken aus der großen Kühlkammer dienen heute als Küchenbar. Nebenan betreiben die Du Vals ihre Landschaftsgärtnerei. Kein Wunder, daß statt Kunst Pflanzen die großen Räume schmücken.

Page précédente: Dans leur fabrique du Queens, les Du Val durent débarrasser les murs de briques des épaisses couches de plâtre et de peinture qui les recouvraient. Les deux halls de séjour sont peu meublés. On ne saurait trouver une seule œuvre d'art au mur dans toute la maison.

Page de gauche: De temps à autre, leur fille Allison joue sur le piano à queue historique de fabrication américaine. Devant, une méridienne. Posé sur une palette de déménagement, l'arbre fragile peut aisément être déplacé d'un endroit à un autre.

Ci-dessus: De la salle à manger on a une vue étonnante sur les fascinants gratte-ciel de Manhattan.

Pages suivantes, à gauche: Grâce à d'anciennes techniques de crépissage, on a pu parfaitement imiter le processus de vieillissement des murs et du bois.

Pages suivantes, à droite : Les propriétaires ont transformé la sordide arrière-cour en un jardin-atrium romantique.

Previous page: In the factory in Queens, multiple layers of plaster and paint had to be stripped from the brick walls. The two vast living rooms are sparsely furnished. The Du Vals have conciously chosen to keep the walls uncluttered.

Facing page: Every now and then their daughter Allison plays the piano, a historically significant American-made instrument. In the foreground is a French daybed. The fragile tree can easily be moved on its industrial four-wheel platform.

Above: The dining room offers a surprising view of the fascinating Manhattan skyline.

Following pages, left: An aging process was perfectly simulated on walls and wood surfaces by means of old cleaning techniques.

Following pages, right: Tim and Dagny Du Val have transformed the unsightly backyard into a romantic atrium-like garden.

Vorhergehende Seite: In dem Fabrikgebäude in Queens mußten dicke Putz- und Farbschichten von den Backsteinwänden heruntergeklopft werden. Die beiden Wohnhallen sind spärlich möbliert. Im ganzen Haus haben die Du Vals auf Kunst an den Wänden verzichtet.

Linke Seite: Auf dem historischen amerikanischen Flügel spielt gelegentlich Tochter Allison, vorne eine Récamiere. Der fragile Baum in dem schweren Terrakottatopf kann auf einer Umzugspalette leicht verschoben werden.

Oben: Aus dem Eßzimmer hat man einen überraschenden Blick auf die faszinierende Skyline von Manhattan.

Folgende Seiten links: Mit alten Putztechniken wurde der Alterungsprozeß von Wänden und Holz perfekt nachgeahmt.

Folgende Seiten rechts: Den früher schäbigen Hinterhof verwandelten die Hauseigentümer in einen romantischen Atriumgarten.

Homme d'affaires aux relations internationales, Asher B. Edelman est toujours à la recherche d'une bonne transaction. Plus l'entreprise est controversée, plus elle l'attire. Sans trêve ni repos, c'est avec la même énergie qu'il s'est constitué sa collection d'œuvres d'art durant les quinze dernières années, et c'est avec la mobilité qui lui est propre qu'il fait faire à ses chefs-d'œuvre de Miró, Picasso, Dubuffet, de Kooning, Holzer, Johns, Rothko, Schnabel, Stella, Twombly, Condo et Kounellis l'aller-retour entre ses domiciles de New York, Paris, Rio et Lausanne. A Lausanne, il s'est érigé un monument public, «The Edelman Foundation Museum for Contemporary Art», construit en 1990 par Jacques Richter. A New York, dans son appartement à terrasse avec vue sur l'East River, le mobilier est, lui aussi, très recherché: entre autres des fauteuils de Josef Hoffmann et un sofa très élégant, fabriqué dans les années 40 pour Christian Dior. «Pied-à-terre», c'est ainsi qu'Edelman désigne son domicile new-yorkais – ce qui est quand même un euphémisme pour un appartement de 1000 m².

Asher B. Edelman

Asher B. Edelman operates businesses worldwide. The more controversial an undertaking, the more attractive it is for him. In the last fifteen years, with the same restless energy, he has assembled his art collection. Displaying characteristic mobility, he shuttles works by artists such as Miró, Picasso, Dubuffet, de Kooning, Holzer, Johns, Rothko, Schnabel, Stella, Twombly, Condo, and Kounellis among his New York, Paris, Rio and Lausanne residences. In Lausanne he opened in 1990 "The Edelman Foundation Museum for Contemporary Art". Looking out over the East River Edelman's New York penthouse harbors his most valuable furniture, such as armchairs by Josef Hoffmann, and an elegant sofa, made for Christian Dior in the 40s. Edelman calls the New York penthouse his *pied à terre*, a brazen understatement for a 1000 sq.m. area.

Asher B. Edelman ist ein weltweit operierender Geschäftsmann, immer auf der Jagd nach dem nächstgrößeren Deal. Je kontroverser ein Geschäft, desto attraktiver ist es für ihn. Mit ähnlich rastloser Energie ist im Laufe der letzten 15 Jahre seine Kunstsammlung entstanden, und mit der ihm eigenen Mobilität schickt er seine Meisterwerke von Miró, Picasso und Dubuffet, von de Kooning, Holzer, Johns, Rothko, Schnabel, Stella, Twombly, Condo und Kounellis zwischen seinen Wohnsitzen in New York, Paris, Rio und Lausanne hin und her. In Lausanne hat er sich ein öffentliches Denkmal gesetzt; sein Museum »The Edelman Foundation Museum for Contemporary Art« wurde 1990 von Jacques Richter erbaut. Auch das Mobiliar seines New Yorker Penthouses mit Blick auf den East River ist vom Feinsten: unter anderem Fauteuils von Josef Hoffmann und ein hochelegantes Sofa, in den 40er Jahren für Christian Dior angefertigt. »Pied à terre«, nennt Edelman sein New Yorker Domizil – eine schamlose Untertreibung für das 1000 m² große Apartment.

Pages précédentes: «Sylvette» de Pablo Picasso, 1964, règne dans la salle de séjour, près d'un banc d'Andrée Putman. A gauche, noir comme les ténèbres, le «Getty Tomb» de Frank Stella, 1969. Sur la photo de détail: derrière le fauteuil de relaxation blanc «Girl with a Purple Dress» de George Condo, 1986.
Ci-dessus: La plaque de verre de la table de la salle à manger repose sur la sculpture arc-en-ciel de George Sugarman, derrière un tableau de néon de Dan Flavin. A gauche, une sculpture en métal de Frank Stella.

Previous pages: Pablo Picasso's "Sylvette", 1964, dominates the living room. Armchair and bench are Andrée Putman designs. On the left is Frank Stella's black "Getty Tomb", 1969. On the detail photo: Behind the white easy chair is George Condo's "Girl with a Purple Dress", 1986.
Above: A glass plate on the dining room table is supported by George Sugarman's rainbow-sculpture. The fluorescent image behind it is by Dan Flavin. To the left is a metal sculpture by Frank Stella.

Vorhergehende Seiten: Im Wohnraum herrscht »Sylvette« von Pablo Picasso. Sessel und Bank von Andrée Putman. Links Frank Stellas nachtschwarzes »Getty Tomb« von 1969. Auf dem Detailfoto: hinter dem weißen Ruhesessel George Condos »Girl with a Purple Dress« von 1986.
Oben: Die Glasplatte des Eßtischs liegt auf der Regenbogen-Skulptur von George Sugarman, dahinter ein Neon-Bild von Dan Flavin. Links eine Metall-Skulptur von Frank Stella.

ABUSE OF POWER COMES AS NO SURPRISE
CLASS ACTION IS A FENCE IDEA WITH A JUSTICE
CLASS STRUCTURE IS AS ARTIFICIAL AS PLASTIC
EATING TOO MUCH IS CRIMINAL
ENJOY YOURSELF BECAUSE YOU CAN'T CHANGE ANYTHING ANYWAY
INHERITANCE MUST BE ABOLISHED
IT IS MAN'S FATE TO OUTSMART HIMSELF
KILLING IS UNAVOIDABLE BUT IS NOTHING TO BE PROUD OF
MOTHERS SHOULDN'T MAKE TOO MANY SACRIFICES
MUCH WAS DECIDED BEFORE YOU WERE BORN
PUSH YOURSELF TO THE LIMIT AS OFTEN AS POSSIBLE
SLIPPING INTO MADNESS IS GOOD FOR THE SAKE OF COMPARISON
THE MOST PROFOUND THINGS ARE INEXPRESSIBLE
THERE'S NOTHING EXCEPT WHAT YOU SENSE
YOU ARE A VICTIM OF THE RULES YOU LIVE BY

IT'S CRUCIAL TO HAVE AN ACTIVE FANTASY LIFE
STUPID PEOPLE SHOULDN'T BREED

ELITE IS INEVITABLE

Page de gauche: une œuvre d'art provocante dans la salle de bains.
Sous les porte-serviettes, le banc «Truisms» – lapalissades – de Jenny
Holzer. Devant, on peut lire entre autres: «STUPID PEOPLE
SHOULDN'T BREED» (les imbéciles ne devraient pas se repro-
duire).
Ci-dessus: La terrasse avec vue sur l'East River communique avec la
bibliothèque. La sculpture-fontaine «Fountain for Asher» de Ben
Jakober perce le ciel.

Facing page: provocative art in the bathroom. Below the towel racks
is Jenny Holzer's bench "Truisms". One of the statements in front
says: "STUPID PEOPLE SHOULDN'T BREED".
Above: A terrace roof adjacent to the library features Ben Jakober's
soaring sculpture "Fountain for Asher".

Linke Seite: provokative Kunst im Bad. Unter Handtuchhaltern
Jenny Holzers Bank mit »Truisms« – Binsenweisheiten. Vorne unter
anderem lesbar: »STUPID PEOPLE SHOULDN´T BREED«
(Dumme Leute sollten sich nicht fortpflanzen).
Oben: Auf der Dachterrasse, die an die Bibliothek anschließt, bohrt
sich die Brunnen-Skulptur »Fountain for Asher« von Ben Jakober in
den Himmel.

Lorsque Robert Franklin, agent de change à Wallstreet, pria son ami l'architecte Manwar Al-Sayed de lui aménager un appartement, il ne lui demanda qu'une seule chose. La nouvelle demeure devait être située dans le centre, mais être en même temps éloignée de l'agitation new-yorkaise. Avec sa partenaire Janet Fink, Al-Sayed transforma l'appartement à terrasse, au dernier étage d'un immeuble des années 20 dans la Fifth Avenue, en un bungalow inondé de lumière. Son point d'attraction est une cour vitrée, ouverte sur le ciel, où le soleil, la neige et la pluie peuvent offrir de véritables spectacles. Presque tous les murs extérieurs ont été remplacés par des façades vitrées, de sorte que l'on peut jouir d'un panorama circulaire sur tout Manhattan. Ce qui peut parfois être dramatique. Les lourds rideaux permettent alors de cacher ce que l'on ne désire pas voir. Au fait: en voulant du calme, Franklin n'était certainement pas sérieux. Sur sa table de nuit, juste à côté de son lit, se trouve un ordinateur Reuters, qui lui livre 24 heures sur 24 les cours actuels de la bourse.

Robert Franklin

When Wall Street broker Robert Franklin asked his friend, the architect Manwar Al-Sayed, to renovate an apartment, he had only one stipulation: it had to be centrally located and yet provide a refuge from the stresses of New York. Al-Sayed and his partner Janet Fink created a lightflooded bungalow in the penthouse apartment of a Fifth Avenue building from the 20s. In the center is a patio, in which sun, snow and rain have free play. The outer walls were almost completely replaced by glass panels, allowing a spectacular 360-degree view of Manhattan. Occasionally this can be too dramatic; then heavy drapes can be drawn to hide the view. Perhaps Franklin's desire for peace and quiet was not so great after all, since a Reuters computer on the night table, right next to his bed, brings round-the-clock updates on stock market prices.

Als Wallstreet-Broker Robert Franklin den befreundeten Architekten Manwar Al-Sayed bat, ein Apartment zu suchen und umzubauen, hatte er eine einzige Vorgabe: Es sollte zentral liegen und trotzdem eine Fluchtmöglichkeit vor der Hektik New Yorks bieten. Mit Partnerin Janet Fink schuf Al-Sayed aus dem Penthouse auf einem Fifth-Avenue-Apartmentgebäude der 20er Jahre einen lichtdurchfluteten Bungalow. Mittelpunkt ist ein zum Himmel geöffneter Lichthof, in dem Sonne, Schnee und Regen ein wahres Wetterleuchten veranstalten können. Die Außenwände wurden beinahe komplett durch Glasfronten ersetzt, so daß sich dem Blick ein 360-Grad-Schauspiel über ganz Manhattan bietet – was gelegentlich sehr dramatisch sein kann. Schwere Vorhänge können auch den Blick ausschließen. Übrigens: Ganz so ernst hat es Franklin wohl mit seiner Sehnsucht nach Ruhe nicht gemeint. Auf seinem Nachttisch, direkt neben seinem Bett, steht ein Reuters-Computer, der ihm rund um die Uhr die aktuellen Börsenkurse liefert.

Premières pages: Soleil et lumière, pluie et neige, tombent dans une cage de bronze, la cour vitrée, qui donne l'impression d'être une sculpture et sépare l'entrée de la salle de séjour.
Double page précédente: S'élevant jusqu'au plafond, la cheminée minimaliste a été construite avec du grès calcaire provenant de la région de Nîmes. Le tableau de Jean-Michel Basquiat a une significa- tion toute particulière: c'est en parlant longuement de l'artiste new- yorkais décédé que les Franklin se sont aperçus qu'ils s'aimaient. Se- lon la méthode vénitienne traditionnelle, les pigments mélangés au stuc fin comme du velours confèrent aux murs de la salle de séjour un bleu ciel intense.
Ci-dessus, à gauche et à droite: Fixé au plafond, le lourd rideau de satin doublé de coton peut être tiré tout autour du lit et le transfor- mer en nid douillet. Le canapé en cuir gris foncé «Diesis» des années 70 vient d'Italie. La baie vitrée à droite donne sur l'une des trois grandes terrasses.
Page de droite: Le marbre italien aux veines blanches et jaunes de la salle de bains fait écho aux matériaux de l'imposant hall d'entrée.

First pages: Sun and light, rain and snow fall into the patio, enclosed by a glass-and-bronze framework, which has the effect of a sculpture separating the entrance from the living area.
Previous pages: The ceiling-high minimalist fireplace was built with a chalky sandstone from the area of Nîmes in southern France. The picture by Jean-Michel Basquiat is of sentimental value: the Franklins discovered their love for each other during a long discussion about this late New York artist. Pigment mixed into fine stucco, a Venetian tra- dition, imparts a deep sky blue to the walls in the living area.

Above left and right: The curtain, heavy brown cotton-lined silk velvet, can be drawn around the bed to make it into a cozy lair. The dark gray "Diesis" leather sofa is 70s Italian. The glass panels to the right open to one of the three large patios.
Facing page: The cool white and yellow Italian marble of the bath- room echoes the materials of the imposing entrance hall.

Erste Seiten: Sonne und Licht, Regen und Schnee fallen in einen ver- glasten Bronze-Käfig, den Lichthof, der wie eine Skulptur wirkt und den Eingangs- vom Wohnbereich trennt.
Vorhergehende Doppelseite: Für den deckenhohen minimalistischen Kamin wurde Kalksandstein aus der Gegend von Nîmes verwendet. Das Bild von Jean-Michel Basquiat hat eine sentimentale Bedeutung: bei einem langen Gespräch über den verstorbenen New Yorker Künst- ler haben die Franklins ihre Liebe zueinander entdeckt. Auf traditio- nelle venezianische Art in den velourfeinen Stuck gemischtes Pigment verleiht den Wänden im Wohnbereich ein tiefes Himmelblau.
Oben links und rechts: Der deckenhohe Vorhang aus schwerem braunen baumwollgefütterten Seidensamt kann rund um das Bett zugezogen werden, es zu einer heimeligen Höhle machen. Das dun- kelgraue 70er-Jahre-Ledersofa »Diesis« stammt aus Italien. Die Glas- front rechts öffnet sich zu einer der drei großen Terrassen.
Rechte Seite: Der kühle weiße und gelbe italienische Marmor des Bades nimmt die Materialien der imposanten Eingangshalle wieder auf.

Attirés par un panneau «For sale», James Gager et Richard Ferretti ont découvert un jour leur duplex de rêve aux cinquième et sixième étages de l'une des rares maisons-ateliers de Greenwich Village qui aient survécu sans trop de mal à la rage de démolition des années 80. Le Senior Vice President et Creative Director de la ligne «Prescriptives» d'Estée Lauder et le Art Director du magazine féminin «Self» aiment l'art moderne et le design, en particulier ceux des années 20 aux années 50. La maison devant laquelle ils aimaient passer au cours de leurs promenades date de 1924, et semble donc prédestinée à abriter toutes les belles œuvres de leur collection. «Mais nous ne nous cramponnons pas», disent-ils. Les objets vont et viennent. Les samedis et dimanches matins sont programmés, quel que soit l'endroit où Gager et Ferretti se trouvent. Pour eux, rien de plus agréable que de fouiner pendant des heures aux puces de New York, Miami et Paris.

James Gager and Richard Ferretti

One day in Greenwich Village, James Gager and Richard Ferretti, guided by a "For Sale" sign high up on a sixth floor, found the duplex of their dreams. It was one of the few lofts which had survived the demolition-frenzy of the 80s almost unscathed. James Gager is Senior Vice President and Creative Director of the Estée Lauder line "Prescriptives", Richard Ferretti is the Art Director of the women's magazine "Self". Both men have a passion for modern art and design, particularly of the 20s to 50s era. The building they discovered dated from 1924 and seemed made for the many objects they had collected. Gager and Ferretti like nothing more than to comb the weekend fleamarkets of New York, Miami and Paris.

In einem der wenigen Atelierhäuser in Greenwich Village, das die Abrißwut der 8oer Jahre beinahe unbeschadet überlebte, haben James Gager und Richard Ferretti eines Tages durch das Schild »For sale« hoch oben im fünften und sechsten Stock ihr Traum-Duplex gefunden. Der Senior Vice President und Creative Director der Estée-Lauder-Linie »Prescriptives« und der Art Director des Frauen-Magazins »Self« lieben Kunst und Design der ersten Hälfte unseres Jahrhunderts, speziell der 2oer bis 5oer Jahre. Das Haus, an dem sie jahrelang immer wieder vorbeispazierten, ist »aus ihrer Zeit«, 1924 erbaut, also prädestiniert für all die schönen Objekte ihrer Sammlung. »Aber wir klammern nicht«, sagen beide. Stücke kommen und gehen. Die Vormittage an den Wochenenden sind schon im voraus verplant – egal, wo sich Gager und Ferretti gerade aufhalten. Für beide gibt es nichts Schöneres, als stundenlang die Flohmärkte von New York, Miami und Paris zu inspizieren.

Première page: La salle de séjour, qui servait autrefois d'atelier, possède un plafond voûté et un mobilier remarquable.
Double page précédente: vue du salon-salle à manger. A partir de la gauche: chaise Bugatti, table de Charlotte Perriand, chaises capitonnées de Jean Royère, lampe spoutnik italienne des années 50, lampadaire Serge Mouille, buffet bas Charlotte Perriand.
Ci-dessus et à droite: Les portraits en noir et blanc des deux caniches royaux Claude et Percy reposent sur la cheminée. De part et d'autre de la cheminée, les lampadaires-lianes de Jean Royère, une petite chaise vénitienne et un paravent américain des années 40.

First page: The living room, converted from an artist's studio, has a vaulted ceiling, and remarkable furniture.
Previous pages: view into the dining room with, from left to right: A Bugatti chair, a dining table by Charlotte Perriand, upholstered chairs by Jean Royère, an Italian Sputnik-lamp from the 50s, a floor-lamp by Serge Mouille, a sideboard by Charlotte Perriand.
Above and right: The fireplace is graced by black and white portraits of giant poodles Claude and Percy. The fireplace is flanked by liana floor lamps, by Jean Royère, a small Venetian chair, and an American composition-board screen dating to the 40s.

Erste Seite: Das Wohnzimmer war früher Künstleratelier und hat eine gewölbte Decke sowie bemerkenswertes Mobiliar.
Vorhergehende Doppelseite: Blick in das Wohn- und Eßzimmer. Von links: Carlo-Bugatti-Stuhl, Eßtisch von Charlotte Perriand, Polsterstühle von Jean Royère, 50er-Jahre-Sputnik-Lampe aus Italien, Stehlampe von Serge Mouille, Sideboard von Charlotte Perriand.
Oben und rechts: Auf dem Kamin Porträts der Pudel Claude und Percy. Den Kamin flankieren die Lianen-Stehlampe von Jean Royère, ein venezianisches Stühlchen und ein amerikanischer 40er-Jahre-Paravent.

A droite: On s'amuse dans la cuisine. La chatte Josephine s'attaque aux fruits. Lampes de Venini.
Ci-dessous: dans la chambre, un lit indien en bois avec de hauts montants. Commode de George Nelson pour Herman Miller; près du lit, un petit tableau de James Wojick. Le grand tableau est l'œuvre du peintre italien contemporain Luigi Campagnelli. Devant, «Swan Chair» d'Arne Jacobsen, 1957.

Right: The kitchen is a pets' paradise – Josephine the cat stalking fruit. The lamps are by Venini.
Below: In the bedroom is a wooden bed with high posts, from India. The chest is by George Nelson for Herman Miller, near the bed is a small picture by James Wojick. The large picture is a work of the Italian contemporary painter Luigi Campagnelli. In front, Arne Jacobsen's "Swan Chair", 1957.

Rechts: tierisches Vergnügen in der Küche: Katze Josephine pirscht sich an die Früchte heran. Lampen von Venini.
Unten: im Schlafzimmer ein indisches Holzbett mit hohen Pfosten. Kommode von George Nelson für Herman Miller, neben dem Bett ein kleines Bild von James Wojick. Das große Gemälde ist ein Werk des italienischen zeitgenössischen Malers Luigi Campagnelli. Vorne Arne Jacobsens »Swan Chair« von 1957.

Malcolm Holzman et sa femme Andrea Landsman habitent sur le toit d'une fabrique de douze étages construite en 1898, avec vue sur les célèbres buildings de New York Life, Metropolitan Life and Con Edison. Partenaire du fameux cabinet d'architecte Hardy Holzman Pfeiffer, Holzman a tenu des cours dans diverses universités et dessiné les plans d'importants musées. Il est un fervent défenseur de l'archéologie et de la culture ouvrière urbaines. Lors de l'aménagement de son loft de 1220 m², il tint absolument à conserver la force primitive qui émanait de la salle-atelier. C'est pourquoi il garda dans leur état d'origine les conduits, les piliers, les plafonds et les fenêtres et utilisa principalement des nouveaux matériaux industriels comme le contreplaqué, le plastique ondulé et le métal bosselé. Pour créer la chambre avec salle de bains et l'entrepôt il a tout simplement compartimenté la pièce. Les œuvres d'artistes célèbres mais aussi celles de parfaits inconnus créent une atmosphère extraordinairement stimulante.

Malcolm Holzman and Andrea Landsman

Malcolm Holzman and his wife Andrea Landsman live in a loft under the roof of a twelve-story industrial building of 1898. They enjoy a view of landmarks such as the New York Life, Metropolitan Life and Con Edison buildings. Malcolm Holzman is a partner in the well-known architectural firm Hardy Holzman Pfeiffer Associates. He has taught at several universities, and designed important museums. Besides avidly supporting urban archeology, he seeks to preserve the cultural history of industry and labor. In his 1220 sq.m. loft he kept the original powerful impact of the workspace intact. Distressed columns, ceilings and wire-glass windows were left in their original state and additions were done primarily in various new industrial materials. Works by legendary and unknown artists create an exciting ambiance.

Malcolm Holzman und seine Frau Andrea Landsman wohnen auf dem Dach eines zwölfstöckigen, 1898 erbauten Industriegebäudes mit Blick auf die berühmten New York Life, Metropolitan Life and Con Edison Buildings. Partner des renommierten Architekturbüros Hardy Holzman Pfeiffer Associates, ehemaliger Professor an verschiedenen Universitäten und unter anderem für den Bau bedeutender Museen verantwortlich, ist Holzman leidenschaftlicher Verfechter urbaner Archäologie und Arbeitskultur. Beim Umbau des 1220 m² großen Lofts sollte die ursprüngliche Kraft des Werkraumes erhalten bleiben. Leitungen, Pfeiler, Decken und Fenster beließ er deshalb im Originalzustand und verwendete vorwiegend neues Industriematerial wie Spanplatten, gewellte Kunststoffplatten und geprägtes Metall. Für Schlafzimmer, Bad und Lager wurden drei freistehende Kästen in den Raum gesetzt. Werke weltbekannter und völlig unbekannter Künstler schaffen eine außergewöhnlich anregende Atmosphäre.

Page précédente: *La vue sur le building illuminé du Metropolitan Life est à couper le souffle. Les murs argentés du loft sont constitués d'un revêtement dont les motifs de briques ont été empreints sur le métal galvanisé. A gauche, un autoportrait de Dana van Horn, un Napoléon tissé recouvre le dos du fauteuil de Morris, sur le rebord de la fenêtre des gratte-ciel en miniature, l'installation vidéo est de Bonnie Erickson.*
Ci-dessus: *La cuisine ouverte a plutôt l'ambiance d'un bar. Les réclames au néon pour la bière Blatz viennent du Wisconsin où Holzman enseignait à la faculté d'architecture. La lampe de table est de Harry Anderson. Derrière le mur et son étagère remplie de souvenirs d'assiettes commémoratives se cachent la chambre, la salle de bains, les toilettes et la penderie.*

Previous page: *The bright lights of the Metropolitan Life Building present a spectacular view. The silvery brick pattern on the walls was stamped into galvanized metal. On the left is a self-portrait by Dana von Horn, a Napoleon tapestry reclines in the Morris armchair, on the window sill stand miniature skyscrapers. The video installation is by Bonnie Erickson.*
Above: *The open kitchen has the atmosphere of a friendly bar. The neon advertisement for Blatz Beer is from Wisconsin, where Holzman taught architecture. The table lamp is by Harry Anderson. Bedroom, bathroom, toilet and dressing rooms are hidden behind the wall, where shelves are crowded with Holzman's collection of souvenir jubilee plates.*

Vorhergehende Seite: *Der Blick auf das hellerleuchtete Metropolitan Life Building ist atemberaubend. Das silbrige Mauerwerk des Lofts ist eine Wandverkleidung aus galvanisiertem Metall mit geprägtem Ziegelsteinmuster. Links ein Selbstporträt von Dana van Horn, ein gewebter Napoleon lehnt in dem Morris-Sessel, auf dem Fenstersims Miniatur-Wolkenkratzer. Die Video-Installation ist von Bonnie Erickson.*
Oben: *Die offene Küche gleicht mehr einer stimmungsvollen Bar. Die Neonreklame für Blatz-Bier stammt aus Wisconsin, wo Holzman an der Universität Architektur lehrte. Die Tischlampe ist von Harry Anderson. Hinter der Wand mit einem Regal voll kurioser Souvenir-Jubiläumsteller verbergen sich Schlafzimmer, Bad, Toilette und Ankleidezimmer.*

Les portes roulantes du garage s'ouvrent sur un entrepôt polyvalent.
Revêtu d'une fibre de verre ondulée savamment éclairée, il se dresse
au milieu du loft comme une maison dans une maison.

Garage doors lead into the multifunctional storage area, which is
built of artfully illuminated corrugated fiberglass and stands in the
center of the loft like a house within a house.

Garagenrolltore führen in den multifunktionalen Lagerraum aus
raffiniert beleuchtetem »Wellblech«-Fiberglas, der wie ein Haus im
Haus mitten in dem Loft steht.

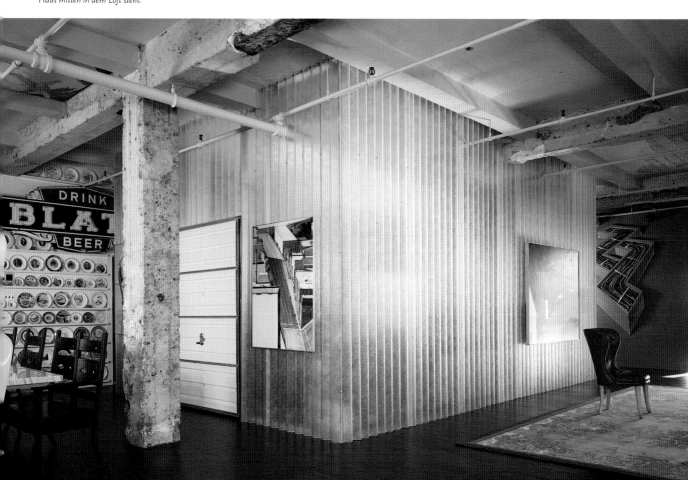

Page de gauche: L'éclairage au néon colore d'un rouge intense les murs en métal. La chaise en contreplaqué peint est d'Alan Siegel. La table standard de Johnson Industries est recouverte d'une plaque en marbre blanc veiné de noir provenant de Georgie.

Ci-dessus, à gauche et à droite: Piliers, plafonds et conduits sont les vestiges de l'architecture industrielle. Accroché au mur vert, un tableau du «Flatiron Building» voisin, réalisé par Daniel Morper, ainsi qu'une sculpture de John O. Kulick; au fond, sur le mur en métal, «Passing Generations» de Roger Brown. L'éclairage mural vient d'une jardinerie.

Double page suivante: sur le sol en bois du séjour, des tapis de Chine tissés à la main; devant à droite, une chaise rare de Josef Hoffmann, vers 1910, fauteuils rembourrés et lampe anthropomorphe de Harry Anderson. Les tableaux sont de Sidney Goodman et de Jack Beal (à droite).

Facing page: Reflected neon bathes the metal walls in a deep red color. The chair of painted plywood is by Alan Siegel. On a standard table by Johnson Industries lies a white black-veined slab of Georgia marble.

Above left and right: Columns, ceiling and pipes are left-overs from the industrial architecture. On the green wall hangs a picture of the neighboring Flatiron Building by Daniel Morper and a sculpture by John O. Kulick; in the background, on the metal wall "Passing Generations" by Roger Brown. The wall lamps are from a garden center.

Following pages: On the wooden floor in the living area are hand-woven Chinese carpets. Right foreground, a rare Josef Hoffmann chair; the easy chair and an anthropomorphic lamp are by Harry Anderson. The pictures are by Sidney Goodman and Jack Beal (right).

Linke Seite: Neonlicht taucht die Metallwände in sattes Rot. Der Stuhl aus bemaltem Sperrholz ist von Alan Siegel. Auf dem Standard-Tisch von Johnson Industries liegt eine weiße schwarzgemaserte Platte aus Georgia-Marmor.

Oben links und rechts: Säulen, Decke und Leitungen sind Überreste der Industriearchitektur. Auf der grünen Wand ein Bild des benachbarten Flatiron Building von Daniel Morper und eine Skulptur von John O. Kulick, hinten auf der Metallwand »Passing Generations« von Roger Brown. Die Wandleuchten stammen aus einem Gartenbedarfsgeschäft.

Folgende Doppelseite: auf dem Holzboden im Wohnbereich handgewebte Teppiche aus China, vorne rechts ein seltener Stuhl von Josef Hoffmann, Polstersessel und eine anthropomorph gestaltete Lampe von Harry Anderson. Die Bilder sind von Sidney Goodman und Jack Beal (rechts).

Cosmopolite de Hambourg et de Postdam, de Monte-Carlo et de Manhattan, le grand couturier et dandy Wolfgang Joop adore son appartement situé dans la Upper East Side de Manhattan qui offre une vue spectaculaire sur la East River. A la fois élégant et extravagant, il dégage une impression de légèreté que l'on trouve rarement dans les appartements sélects de New York. Dans le salon bleu pâle, des pièces uniques des années 40 et 50 signées Jean Prouvé et Jean Royère content fleurette à une commode vénitienne du 18e siècle. Dans la chambre blanche, Joop a réuni les ouvrages d'artistes et designers internationaux. Un paravent de l'Américain John Risley, une sculpture en bois du Français Alexandre Noll, des tables en bois de George Nakashima, des lampes de Serge Mouille, des chaises d'Arne Jacobsen. Ses tableaux fantastiques de Tamara de Lempicka et sa remarquable collection de photos de Irving Penn et Robert Mapplethorpe ajoutent une note subtile de décadence.

Wolfgang Joop

Wolfgang Joop, cosmopolitan fashion designer and dandy from Hamburg and Potsdam, Monte Carlo and Manhattan, adores his penthouse apartment on Manhattan's Upper East Side and its spectacular view of the East River. The atmosphere is elegant and extravagant but with an insouciance not often seen in apartments of the New York elite. The salon walls are washed in pastel blue, highlighting superb 40s and 50s Paris pieces by Jean Prouvé and Jean Royère. In the white bedroom, Joop keeps works by a highly individual group of international artists and designers: a screen by American John Risley, a wooden sculpture by Alexandre Noll of France, wooden tables by George Nakashima, lamps by Serge Mouille, and chairs by Arne Jacobsen. Joop's fantastic Tamara de Lempicka paintings and Irving Penn and Robert Mapplethorpe photos add a touch of decadence.

Wolfgang Joop, Weltbürger aus Hamburg und Potsdam, Monte Carlo und Manhattan, Modedesigner und Dandy, ist in sein Penthouse an der Upper East Side von Manhattan mit spektakulärem Blick über den East River geradezu vernarrt. Die Atmosphäre ist elegant und extravagant und zugleich von einer Leichtigkeit, die man in New Yorker Upper-Class-Wohnungen nicht oft findet. Im blaßblau getünchten Salon bezaubern erlesene Einzelstücke aus dem Paris der 4oer und 5oer Jahre von Jean Prouvé und Jean Royère vor einer venezianischen Kommode aus dem 18. Jahrhundert. Im weißen Schlafzimmer hat Joop eine eigenwillige Melange internationaler Künstler und Designer versammelt. Ein Paravent des Amerikaners John Risley, eine Holzskulptur des Franzosen Alexandre Noll, Holztische von George Nakashima, Lampen von Serge Mouille, Stühle von Arne Jacobsen. Einen Hauch von feiner Dekadenz verströmen Joops phantastische Gemälde von Tamara de Lempicka und seine bemerkenswerte Fotosammlung von Irving Penn und Robert Mapplethorpe.

Un mas provençal avec un petit air new-yorkais. C'est ce qu'est devenue l'ancienne fabrique de chocolats à SoHo après les transformations que lui ont fait subir Laurence et William Kriegel pour abriter
leur famille de cinq enfants. Surface totale: 1850 m² répartis sur
4 étages. Laurence Kriegel – qui possède le magasin de décoration
«Intérieurs» dans la Wooster Street – est née en Angleterre et a
grandi dans les brumes du Nord-Ouest de la France. Il y a quelques
années, visitant le Midi, elle a été fascinée par la luminosité et les
matériaux de la Provence. C'est ainsi qu'elle a trouvé en France tout
ce dont elle avait besoin pour créer à New York une atmosphère provençale. Des containers remplis de matériaux de construction et
d'antiquités ont été expédiés à New York: portes anciennes, fontaines
en pierre, sacs contenant des pigments de couleur abricot, carreaux
en terre cuite par centaines. Seul le plancher en bois grinçant vient de
granges abandonnées du Massachusetts. Quant au vieux château
d'eau, on ne saurait s'y méprendre, il est typiquement new yorkais.

Laurence Kriegel

For themselves and their five children, Laurence and William
Kriegel transformed what was once a SoHo chocolate factory into a
provençal country home with New York flair. Their total living area
is 1850 sq.m. on four floors. Laurence Kriegel runs the decorator
shop "Intérieurs" on Wooster Street. She was born in England and
grew up in the rugged northwest of France. Exploring the south of
France a few years ago on a Harley Davidson, she was captivated
by the light and the materials of Provence. Then began a search for
everything needed to create the most authentic Provençal atmosphere possible in New York. Containers full of building materials
and antiques, doors, stone fountains, wrought-iron gates, sacks
full of apricot-colored pigment, and hundreds of old ceramic tiles
arrived. Only the floorboards are from abandoned barns in Massachusetts, and the old water tower is clearly original New York.

Eine ehemalige Schokoladenfabrik in SoHo haben Laurence und William Kriegel für sich und ihre fünf Kinder in ein provenzalisches Landhaus mit New-York-Flair umgewandelt. Gesamtwohnfläche: 1850 m²
auf vier Etagen. Laurence Kriegel – sie betreibt in der Wooster Street
das Dekorationsgeschäft »Intérieurs« – ist in England geboren und
im rauhen Nordwestfrankreich aufgewachsen. Seit sie vor wenigen
Jahren auf einem Motorrad zum ersten Mal den Süden Frankreichs
bereiste, hat sie die Faszination von Licht und Materialien der Provence nicht mehr losgelassen. Und so suchte und fand sie in Frankreich alles, um in New York eine möglichst authentische Atmosphäre
schaffen zu können. Container mit Baumaterial und Antiquitäten
wurden nach New York verschifft: alte Türen, Steinbrunnen, schmiedeeiserne Gartentore, Säcke mit apricotfarbenem Pigment, Hunderte
von alten Terrakottafliesen. Nur die knarrenden Holzdielen kommen
aus verlassenen Scheunen in Massachusetts. Und der alte Wasserturm ist unverkennbar original New York.

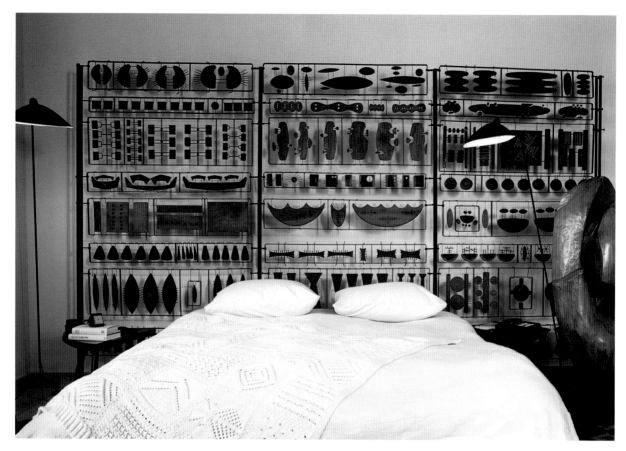

Pages précédentes: des murs bleu ciel et une cheminée dorée dans le séjour. Une mosaïque en verre de Gruppo Bisazza. Les sculptures en bois sur la cheminée sont d'Alexandre Noll, la photo est d'Irving Penn. Les fauteuils ont été fabriqués par Jean Royère. La photo de mode d'Irving Penn est éclairée par un lampadaire en acier, en forme de lianes, de Royère. Au-dessus de la console du 18e siècle, «La fille à l'ours en peluche», 1940, de Tamara de Lempicka. Tout autour, une collection de meubles français des années 50. Fauteuil, sofa et tabouret de Jean Royère, table en acier et terrazzo de Jean Prouvé; dessus, un vase en céramique de F. Carlton Ball. A gauche du passage, un chandelier en fer, 1910, de Marie Zimmerman.

Ci-dessus: à la tête du lit de Joop un paravent en bois et acier réalisé en 1957 par l'artiste américain John Risley. A droite et à gauche du lit, une table en noyer de George Nakashima; à droite, une énorme sculpture en bois d'Alexandre Noll. Dessus de lit en coton de Portico, lampes de Serge Mouille.

Page de droite: dans le bureau de Joop, une table en chêne des années 50 signée Charlotte Perriand. Chaises en cuir et en acier de Jean Prouvé. Lampadaire à trois bras de Serge Mouille.

Previous pages: Sky-blue walls set off a golden fireplace made of glass mosaic in the living room. The wooden sculptures on the mantel are by Alexandre Noll, the photo by Irving Penn. The easy chairs are by Jean Royère. Above the golden Venetian console table from the 18th century hangs "Girl with Teddybear", 1940, by Tamara de Lempicka. Joop's collection includes French furniture from the 50s. Armchair, sofa and stool by Jean Royère, on the terrazzo and steel table by Jean Prouvé stands a ceramic vase by F. Carlton Ball. Left of the doorway an iron candelabra, 1910, by Marie Zimmerman.

Above: A wood and steel screen by American artist John Risley from 1957 functions as the headboard for Joop's bed. The flanking walnut night tables are by George Nakashima, an enormous wooden sculpture by Noll, lamps by Serge Mouille.

Facing page: in Joop's studio the 50s oak desk by Charlotte Perriand, in front leather and steel chairs by Jean Prouvé. The floor lamp with three extensions is by Serge Mouille.

Vorhergehende Seiten: himmelblaue Wände und ein goldener Kamin aus Glasmosaik im Wohnraum. Die Holzskulpturen auf dem Kaminsims sind von Alexandre Noll, das Foto ist von Irving Penn. Über dem vergoldeten venezianischen Konsoltisch aus dem 18. Jahrhundert »Mädchen mit Teddybär« von Tamara de Lempicka von 1940. Dazu eine Sammlung französischer Möbel aus den 50er Jahren: Sessel, Sofa und Hocker von Jean Royère, Tisch aus Terrazzo und Stahl von Jean Prouvé, darauf eine Keramikvase von F. Carlton Ball. Links neben dem Durchgang ein Eisenleuchter von Marie Zimmerman von 1910.

Oben: am Kopfende von Joops Bett ein Paravent aus Holz und Stahl des amerikanischen Künstlers John Risley von 1957. Rechts und links zwei Tische aus Walnußholz von George Nakashima, rechts eine gewaltige Holzskulptur von Alexandre Noll, Lampen von Serge Mouille.

Rechte Seite: in Joops Arbeitszimmer ein 50er-Jahre-Schreibtisch aus Eichenholz von Charlotte Perriand, davor Leder- und Stahlstühle von Jean Prouvé. Dreiarmige Stehlampe von Serge Mouille.

Un mas provençal avec un petit air new-yorkais. C'est ce qu'est devenue l'ancienne fabrique de chocolats à SoHo après les transformations que lui ont fait subir Laurence et William Kriegel pour abriter leur famille de cinq enfants. Surface totale: 1850 m² répartis sur 4 étages. Laurence Kriegel – qui possède le magasin de décoration «Intérieurs» dans la Wooster Street – est née en Angleterre et a grandi dans les brumes du Nord-Ouest de la France. Il y a quelques années, visitant le Midi, elle a été fascinée par la luminosité et les matériaux de la Provence. C'est ainsi qu'elle a trouvé en France tout ce dont elle avait besoin pour créer à New York une atmosphère provençale. Des containers remplis de matériaux de construction et d'antiquités ont été expédiés à New York: portes anciennes, fontaines en pierre, sacs contenant des pigments de couleur abricot, carreaux en terre cuite par centaines. Seul le plancher en bois grinçant vient de granges abandonnées du Massachusetts. Quant au vieux château d'eau, on ne saurait s'y méprendre, il est typiquement new yorkais.

Laurence Kriegel

For themselves and their five children, Laurence and William Kriegel transformed what was once a SoHo chocolate factory into a provençal country home with New York flair. Their total living area is 1850 sq.m. on four floors. Laurence Kriegel runs the decorator shop "Intérieurs" on Wooster Street. She was born in England and grew up in the rugged northwest of France. Exploring the south of France a few years ago on a Harley Davidson, she was captivated by the light and the materials of Provence. Then began a search for everything needed to create the most authentic Provençal atmosphere possible in New York. Containers full of building materials and antiques, doors, stone fountains, wrought-iron gates, sacks full of apricot-colored pigment, and hundreds of old ceramic tiles arrived. Only the floorboards are from abandoned barns in Massachusetts, and the old water tower is clearly original New York.

Eine ehemalige Schokoladenfabrik in SoHo haben Laurence und William Kriegel für sich und ihre fünf Kinder in ein provenzalisches Landhaus mit New-York-Flair umgewandelt. Gesamtwohnfläche: 1850 m² auf vier Etagen. Laurence Kriegel – sie betreibt in der Wooster Street das Dekorationsgeschäft »Intérieurs« – ist in England geboren und im rauhen Nordwestfrankreich aufgewachsen. Seit sie vor wenigen Jahren auf einem Motorrad zum ersten Mal den Süden Frankreichs bereiste, hat sie die Faszination von Licht und Materialien der Provence nicht mehr losgelassen. Und so suchte und fand sie in Frankreich alles, um in New York eine möglichst authentische Atmosphäre schaffen zu können. Container mit Baumaterial und Antiquitäten wurden nach New York verschifft: alte Türen, Steinbrunnen, schmiedeeiserne Gartentore, Säcke mit apricotfarbenem Pigment, Hunderte von alten Terrakottafliesen. Nur die knarrenden Holzdielen kommen aus verlassenen Scheunen in Massachusetts. Und der alte Wasserturm ist unverkennbar original New York.

Premières pages: *Sous l'ancienne citerne caractéristique de New York, un baquet géant en bois de cèdre, se trouve la maison de bains; les portes cintrées s'ouvrent sur un vaste jardin suspendu. Les éléments de la salle de bain sont en bois de pin, le lavabo et la baignoire en grès français. Du couloir, on voit la salle à manger. Les carreaux de terre cuite ont été importées de France.*
Double page précédente: *Le château d'eau abrite un petit salon intime. Le soleil couchant jette ses dernières lueurs sur Manhattan.*
Ci-dessus: *La grille française en fer forgé date du 19e siècle. Le tableau aux tasses et aux assiettes est de Tellurs. Par l'escalier, on accède aux chambres à coucher du second étage.*

First pages: *Beneath the typical old New York water tower, a huge cedar wood tank, is a new bathhouse with arched doors opening into a large roof garden. In the bathroom, pine was used for the built-in elements, French sandstone for sink and bathtub. View from the living area into the dining room. The ceramic floor tiles were imported from France.*
Previous pages: *Concealed in the water tower is an intimate salon. Manhattan's skyline gleams in the evening sun.*
Above: *The French wrought-iron garden gate is from the 19th century, the cups-and-saucers picture is by Tellurs. The stairs lead up into the sleeping area on the second floor of the loft.*

Erste Seiten: *Unter dem alten typischen New Yorker Wasserreservoir, einem riesigen Bottich aus Zedernholz, ist das Badehaus eingebaut; die Bogentüren führen auf einen großen Dachgarten. Die Einbauten im Bad sind aus Kiefer, Waschbecken und Badewanne aus französischem Sandstein. Durchblick von der Diele in das Eßzimmer. Die Terracotta-Fliesen wurden aus Frankreich importiert.*
Vorhergehende Doppelseite: *Im Wasserturm ist ein kleiner, intimer Salon untergebracht. In der Abendsonne leuchtet Manhattan.*
Oben: *Das schmiedeeiserne französische Gartentor stammt aus dem 19. Jahrhundert, das Teller- und Tassen-Bild ist von Tellurs. Die Treppe führt hinauf in den Schlafbereich im zweiten Stock des Lofts.*

Des fauteuils et des sofas blancs et moelleux dans le séjour; au plafond, le système d'aération en zinc décrit ses méandres entre les
poutres de bois. Les fauteuils et le banc en bois de teck mat sont des
reproductions d'originaux français; le lampadaire Lieux vient de Paris.
Le plancher en bois provient de vieilles granges du Massachusetts.

White soft easy chairs in the living area. Exposed ventilation ducts
snake across the beamed ceiling. Matte-finish teak armchairs and
bench are reproductions of French originals, the Lieux floor lamp
comes from Paris. The wooden floorboards hail from old barns in
Massachusetts.

Weiche, weiße Sessel im Wohnbereich, an der Decke schlängelt sich
das Lüftungssystem aus Zink. Die Sessel und die Bank aus mattem
Teakholz sind Nachbauten französischer Originale, die Lieux-Steh-
lampe ist aus Paris. Die Holzdielen stammen aus alten Scheunen in
Massachusetts.

Page de gauche et ci-dessus: jeux de lumière dans la chambre. Les persiennes ont été faites avec d'anciennes lattes de plancher. A travers les jours en forme de fleurs, les rayons du soleil jettent des bouquets lumineux sur le lit des parents. Le fauteuil finement sculpté aux incrustations de nacre, la table et l'encensoir viennent du Maroc; le lampadaire est de Fortuny.
A droite: Les murs de la chambre et de la salle de bain sont recouverts d'un fin ciment jaune et gris.

Facing page and above: The bedroom window shutters are made of antique floorboards whose carved floral designs throw bouquets of sunrays onto the parents' bed. The delicately carved folding chair includes mother-of-pearl inlay, the table and incense vessels are from Morocco, the floor lamp is by Fortuny.
Right: The walls in the bed- and bathroom areas are done in smooth yellow and gray cement.

Linke Seite und oben: Lichtspiele im Schlafzimmer. Die Fensterläden sind alte Bodendielen, durch die stilisierten floralen Schnitzereien fallen Bouquets von Sonnenstrahlen auf das elterliche Bett. Der feingeschnitzte Scherensessel mit Perlmuttintarsien, der Tisch und die Weihrauchgefäße stammen aus Marokko, die Stehlampe ist von Fortuny.
Rechts: Die Wände im Schlaf- und Badebereich sind aus feinem Zement, in Gelb und Grau getüncht.

Dans l'agitation new-yorkaise et à l'aube du 21e siècle, David McDermott et Peter McGough se refusent énergiquement à entrer dans la vie moderne. Extravagants, bourrés de succès, les deux hommes qui sont à la fois photographes, peintres, artistes de performances et dandys, ont arrêté le temps: ils sont fin 19e jusqu'au bout des doigts. Leur maison construite en 1896, une ancienne banque située dans une petite rue tranquille de Brooklyn, est l'oasis idéale. «Regardez donc cette vie d'aujourd'hui. Le monde n'est qu'un chaos hurlant et puant sur le point d'exploser», constate McGough avec irritation. Ils circulent à pied, par principe, et n'utilisent que rarement leur Ford T, un élégant oldtimer. Leurs peintures et photographies – réalisées avec des appareils, des accessoires et des costumes d'origine – révèlent souvent avec verdeur des aspects socio-critiques de la société. Alors, modernes, quand même?

David McDermott and Peter McGough

Amidst the hectic routine of New York on the threshold of the 21st century, David McDermott and Peter McGough maintain a passionate unconcern. The successful photographers, painters and performers have turned the clock back to the *fin de siècle*. Their Brooklyn home, a former bank built in 1896, is the perfect oasis for their experiment in time. "The world today is one screaming, stinking chaos, ready to explode," says the exasperated McGough. But how keep chaos at bay? They insist on walking everywhere, only rarely using their Model-T Ford. In their pictures and photographs, they use original cameras, props and costumes. Often their works are critical of social conditions – a modern couple after all?

Im hektischen New Yorker Alltag auf der Schwelle zum 21. Jahrhundert weigern sich David McDermott und Peter McGough leidenschaftlich, an jeglichem modernen Leben teilzunehmen. Die extravaganten und äußerst erfolgreichen Fotografen, Maler, Performer und Dandys halten konsequent die Zeit an – ungefähr im ausgehenden 19. Jahrhundert. Sie sind perfekt kultiviert bis hin zu Kleidung, Frisur und Aussprache. Ihr 1896 erbautes Haus, eine ehemalige Bank in einer ruhigen Seitenstraße von Brooklyn, ist die perfekte Oase für ihr Zeitexperiment. »Sehen Sie sich dieses Leben doch an. Die Welt heute ist ein einziges schreiendes, stinkendes Chaos kurz vor der Explosion«, erregt sich McGough – ein Chaos, das sie an ihr Leben nicht heranlassen. Sie gehen prinzipiell zu Fuß, nur selten benutzen sie ihren Model-T-Ford, einen eleganten Oldtimer. Ihre Bilder und Fotografien, die mit historischen Originalkameras, Requisiten und Kostümen detailbesessen in Szene gesetzt sind, zeigen oft deftige sozialkritische Aspekte. Eben doch ein modernes Paar.

Premières pages: David McDermott et Peter McGough vivent et travaillent dans les locaux d'une ancienne banque à Brooklyn. Construite en 1896, leur maison illustre parfaitement l'architecture Empire tardive new-yorkaise. Dans certaines pièces, on a conservé les somptueuses boiseries d'origine. A l'étage supérieur, l'atelier a 7 m de haut.
Page double précédente: bienvenue en cette fin du 19e siècle. Au premier étage, la fabuleuse salle de séjour aux teintes de bleuet donne sur un balcon surplombant l'entrée imposante de l'ancienne banque. Tableaux de McDermott/McGough. A gauche, le gramophone n'est nullement une décoration, il fonctionne parfaitement. Les deux artistes refusent tout ce qui est moderne, donc aussi télévision et lecteurs de disques compacts.
Ci-dessus: La décoration du salon rouge est composée essentiellement d'accessoires de théâtre du 19e siècle, affiches peintes à la main, costumes, fragments de décors.
Page de droite: Les artistes travaillent avec des appareils-photos anciens dans des boîtiers en bois. Leur collection comprend 20 appareils, tous en parfait état.

First pages: David McDermott and Peter McGough live and work in an old bank building in Brooklyn. Built in 1896, the house is a perfect example of late New York Empire architecture. A few of the rooms still have the splendid original wall paneling. The upper-floor studio is almost 7 m high.
Previous pages: Welcome to the late 19th century. The imposing cornflower-blue living room on the first floor opens to a balcony above the palatial former bank entrance. The pictures are by McDermott/McGough. The gramophone on the left is not a mere decoration but plays very well. Both artists reject all modern amenities, including CD-player and television set.

Above: For the most part the furnishings in the red salon are 19th-century theater properties, handpainted backdrops, costumes and stage-set fragments.
Facing page: The artists work with antique cameras in wooden housings. Their collection contains 20 cameras, all optically and technically in perfect condition.

Erste Seiten: David McDermott und Peter McGough leben und arbeiten in einem alten Bankgebäude in Brooklyn. 1896 erbaut ist das Haus ein perfektes Beispiel später New Yorker Empire-Architektur. In einigen Räumen sind die prachtvollen Wandtäfelungen im Original erhalten. Das Atelier im oberen Stock ist 7 m hoch.
Vorhergehende Doppelseite: Willkommen im späten 19. Jahrhundert. Die fabelhafte kornblumenblaue Wohnhalle im ersten Stock öffnet sich zu einem Balkon über dem imposanten ehemaligen Bankeingang. Gemälde von McDermott und McGough. Das Grammophon links ist keineswegs Dekoration, sondern absolut funktionstüchtig. Die beiden Künstler lehnen alles Moderne ab, also auch CD-Player und Fernseher.
Oben: Die Einrichtungsstücke im roten Salon sind größtenteils Requisiten aus dem 19. Jahrhundert, handgemalte Theaterprospekte und Kostüme, Fragmente von Bühnenbauten.
Rechte Seite: Die Künstler arbeiten mit historischen Kameras in Holzgehäusen. Ihre Sammlung umfaßt 20 Apparate, alle optisch und technisch in perfektem Zustand.

Page de gauche: devant l'affiche de théâtre représentant des éléphants parés de bijoux dans un décor de jungle indienne, un caisson vitré avec des oiseaux exotiques empaillés et un autre avec des écureils. Kaftan et turban sur le mannequin en fer complètent l'agencement mi-oriental, mi-paradisiaque.

Ci-dessus: Sur une tapisserie drapée avec art se trouvent les plus belles pièces de leur collection d'anciennes chaussures, témoins d'un savoir artisanal que ne maîtrisent plus aujourd'hui que quelques cordonniers dans le monde.

Facing page: In front of the theater backdrop depicting jewel-encrusted elephants in the midst of an Indian jungle landscape, stand a terrarium with stuffed exotic birds and another with squirrels. Kaftan and turban on an iron clothes dummy complete the idyllic oriental arrangement.

Above: On an artfully draped Gobelin stand the finest pieces from their collection of antique shoes, testimony of a craftsmanship mastered by only a handful of shoemakers in the entire world.

Linke Seite: vor dem Theaterprospekt, der juwelenbehangene Elefanten inmitten einer indischen Dschungellandschaft zeigt, ein Terrarium mit ausgestopften exotischen Vögeln, ein anderes mit Eichhörnchen. Kaftan und Turban auf einer eisernen Kleiderpuppe vervollständigen das paradiesisch-orientalische Arrangement.

Oben: Auf einem kunstvoll drapierten Gobelin stehen die schönsten Stücke ihrer Sammlung alter, wertvoller Schuhe, Zeugen einer Handwerkskunst, die heute nur noch eine Handvoll Schuhmacher auf der ganzen Welt beherrscht.

Rentrant chez lui, le peintre et architecte Steve Mensch vit un jour un groupe d'étudiants en architecture en train de dessiner l'étrange façade de sa maison. Invités à pénétrer dans la demeure construite au 19e siècle dans le style roman, les jeunes gens trouvèrent un monde tout en contraste, composé d'arbres, de lumière, d'architecture moderne et de technologie sophistiquée. La grande cour intérieure peut rester ouverte par mauvais temps; son toit en verre amovible permet de l'utiliser toute l'année. Le sol en granit cache un chauffage par le sol. Un ordinateur commande les systèmes de la lumière, du toit, de la fontaine, des stores et du chevalet escamotable – il disparaît dans le sol – sur lequel Mensch peut déplacer à son gré ses tableaux grand format. Le sol de la piscine en dalles de verre sert de source lumineuse à l'appartement du dessous. Un étudiant finit par demander: «Et où se trouve votre Batmobil, s'il vous plaît?». Mensch passe la moitié de la semaine avec sa famille dans une vieille ferme de Pennsylvanie. Voilà un homme qui aime les contrastes.

Steve Mensch

Steve Mensch, architect and painter, returned home one day to find a group of architecture students sketching the dense, mysterious façade of his Manhattan home, where a modern, windowless building can be glimpsed through a 19th-century Romanesque "ruin". Invited in, the students found a constrasting world of trees, light, modern architecture and exceptional technology. The large central court can be left open, but also has a sliding glass roof which permits year-round use. A central computer controls lights, sound, roof, fountain, sun-shades, shutters and the motorized easel which lowers large canvases through a slot in the studio floor. Glass blocks on the pool floor provide light for the office below. One student asked: "Where do you keep the batmobile?" For half the week, Mensch lives with his family in an old stone farmhouse in rural Pennsylvania. A life richer in contrast is hard to imagine.

Als Steve Mensch, Architekt und Maler, eines Tages nach Hause kam, saß vor der neoromanischen Fassade seines im 19. Jahrhundert erbauten Hauses eine Gruppe von Architekturstudenten und fertigte eifrig Skizzen an. Die zur Besichtigung eingeladenen Studenten fanden eine gegensätzliche Welt aus Bäumen, Licht, moderner Architektur und außergewöhnlicher Technik vor. Der große Innenhof kann bei Regen und Schnee geöffnet bleiben, hat aber auch ein bewegliches Glasdach, das eine Nutzung während des ganzes Jahres ermöglicht. Der Granitfußboden ist mit einer Fußbodenheizung ausgestattet. Ein zentraler Computer steuert Licht, Dach, Brunnen, Sonnen- und Sichtblenden sowie die im Studioboden versenkbare Staffelei, auf der Mensch seine großformatigen Bilder nach Belieben bewegen kann. Der Poolboden aus Glasbausteinen ist Lichtquelle für das darunterliegende Büro. Es fragte ein Student kopfschüttelnd: »Und wo bitte ist Ihr Batmobil?« Die Hälfte der Woche lebt Steve Mensch mit seiner Familie in einem alten Farmhaus auf dem Land in Pennsylvania. Kontrastreicher kann Leben kaum sein.

Pages précédentes: Dans une petite rue tranquille de Manhattan, une rareté architectonique se cache derrière la façade d'une maison: une cour intérieure de 12 m de long sur 6 m de large sépare deux pavillons aériens de deux étages. Le premier abrite l'atelier de l'architecte et peintre new-yorkais Steve Mensch, le second son appartement. Dans le séjour, un canapé et chaise longue italiens, dans la chambre un fauteuil de relaxation de Le Corbusier.
Ci-dessus: Le sol de la piscine est en carreaux de verre et sert de plafond à l'appartement du dessous.
Page de droite: vue de l'atelier de Steve Mensch. Une très vieille table roulante de dentiste et un seau à champagne des années 20 contiennent aujourd'hui les pinceaux et les outils du peintre. A droite, dans l'entrée qui mène à l'atelier, une statue birmane en grès de Vishnou, début du 11e siècle.

Previous pages: Hiding behind a Romanesque style ruined façade in a quiet side street of Manhattan is an interesting architectural rarity, two airy two-story pavilions separated by an almost 12 m long and 6 m wide interior court. New York architect and painter Steve Mensch made one pavilion to serve as his studio, the other as his apartment. In the living area, the sofa and couch are from Italy. The chair in the bedroom is by Le Corbusier.

Above and facing page: The pool floor is made of glass bricks and doubles as a skylight for the apartment below. A view of Steve Mensch's studio: an antique dentist's instrument cart and a champagne cooler from the 20s hold his brushes and painting material. To the right of the studio entrance is a kneeling Burmese sandstone Vishnu-statue from the early 11th century.

Vorhergehende Seiten: Hinter der Ruinenfassade in einer ruhigen Seitenstraße Manhattans verbirgt sich eine interessante architektonische Rarität: zwei durch einen 12 m langen und 6 m breiten Innenhof getrennte, luftige, zweistöckige Pavillons. In dem einen das Atelier des Architekten und Malers Steve Mensch, im anderen seine Wohnung. Der Wohnraum ist ausgestattet mit einem Sofa und einer Chaiselongue aus Italien, das Schlafzimmer mit einer Le-Corbusier-Liege.
Oben: Der Boden des Pools besteht aus Glasbausteinen und dient gleichzeitig als Oberlicht für das darunterliegende Apartment.
Rechte Seite: Blick in das Atelier von Steve Mensch. In dem historischen Instrumentenwagen eines Zahnarztes und in einem Champagnerkühler aus den 20er Jahren stecken heute Pinsel und Werkzeuge des Malers. Rechts im Eingang zum Atelier sitzt eine burmesische Vishnu-Statue aus Sandstein aus dem frühen 11. Jahrhundert.

Vue de l'atelier de Mensch, depuis la chambre et au-dessus de la cour intérieure. Mensch fit tisser le tapis par un artisan mexicain, d'après un dessin qu'il avait réalisé lors d'un voyage au Mexique. En bas sur la terrasse devant l'atelier, un exemplaire non verni, en hêtre et contreplaqué, de la «Chaise rouge-bleu» de Gerrit Thomas Rietveld.

View from the bedroom across the interior court to Mensch's studio. The carpet was made by a Mexican weaver from a sketch done by Mensch while travelling there. Below on the terrace, to the right in front of the studio is an unpainted chair of beechwood and plywood, "Red-Blue Chair", by Gerrit Thomas Rietveld.

Blick vom Schlafzimmer über den Innenhof in das Atelier. Den Teppich fertigte ein mexikanischer Weber nach einer Skizze, die Mensch auf einer Reise nach Mexiko entwarf. Unten auf der Terrasse vor dem Atelier ein unlackiertes Exemplar von Gerrit Thomas Rietvelds »Rot-Blau-Stuhl« aus Buchen- und Sperrholz.

Steve Mensch consacre de plus en plus de temps à sa passion, la peinture, notamment celle de corps athlétiques. Le lutteur sumo est l'une
de ses œuvres. La sculpture à droite est la reproduction de la «Victoire
de Samothrace» dont l'original se trouve au Louvre. A gauche, une
maquette de la maison. Le vase sur la table est un objet artisanal
anglais; les chaises sont de Mario Bellini.

Steve Mensch dedicates an increasing amount of time to painting,
especially the painting of athletic figures. The Sumo wrestler is one of
his works. The bronze sculpture on the right is a scaled-down version
of the "Winged Victory" in the Louvre in Paris. On the left is a model
of the house. The vase on the dining table is turn-of-the-century English Arts and Crafts, the chairs are by Mario Bellini.

Steve Mensch widmet immer mehr Zeit der Malerei. Seine Passion
gilt der Darstellung von athletischen Körpern. Der Sumo-Ringer ist
sein Werk. Die Skulptur rechts eine die Nachbildung der »Nike von
Samothrake«, die sich im Pariser Louvre befindet. Links ein Modell
des Hauses. Die Vase auf dem Eßtisch ist englisches Kunstgewerbe,
die Stühle sind von Mario Bellini.

Ci-dessus: Sur le toit d'un immeuble des années 30, une terrasse de 200 m² jouxte le salon de Milhaupt. Paravent en contre-plaqué lamellé et chaise LCW de Charles et Ray Eames, canapé de T.H. Robsjohn-Gibbings. Sur la cheminée, quatre vases Skyscraper de Coors Ceramics, 1930.
Page de droite: le polaroïd «Crowned» de William Wegman, 1991, au-dessus d'un petit cabinet conçu par Kem Weber en 1932 pour les studios Walt Disney à Burbank; à gauche, vase et lampadaire Memphis d'Ettore Sottsass. Devant, un fauteuil Paul Frankl et une petite table Noguchi.

Oben: An den Salon von Milhaupts Penthouse auf dem Dach eines 30er-Jahre-Gebäudes schließt sich eine 200 m² große Terrasse an. Der Paravent aus schichtverleimtem Sperrholz und der LCW-Stuhl sind von Charles und Ray Eames, das Sofa von T.H. Robsjohn-Gibbings. Auf dem Kaminsims vier Skyscraper-Vasen von Coors Ceramics von 1930.
Rechte Seite: Das William-Wegman-Polaroid »Crowned« von 1991 hängt über einem Kabinettschränkchen, das Kem Weber 1932 für die Walt Disney Studios in Burbank entwarf. Links eine Memphis-Vase und -Stehlampe von Ettore Sottsass, davor ein Paul-Frankl-Sessel und ein Tischchen von Isamu Noguchi.

Above: The salon in Milhaupt's penthouse apartment on the roof of a building from the 30s is connected to a 200 sq.m. terrace and is furnished with a screen of cemented layers of plywood, a laminated wood LCW chair by Charles and Ray Eames, and a sofa by T.H. Robsjohn-Gibbings. On the mantel are four skyscraper vases by Coors Ceramics, 1930.
Facing page: A 1991 polaroid "Crowned" by William Wegman hangs above a small cabinet, designed by Kem Weber, 1932, for Walt Disney Studios in Burbank. The Memphis vase and floorlamp are by Ettore Sottsass. Before them a Paul Frankl armchair and a small Isamu Noguchi table.

New York Interiors   Charles M. Milhaupt

Fidéicommissaire de la Fondation philanthropique Howard-Gilman, Charles M. Milhaupt a grandi en Californie avant d'entrer dans le monde du cinéma. Il a un faible pour les films américains des années 30 et 40. Ce n'est donc pas un hasard si son trois-pièces de 240 m², situé dans un immeuble des années 30 de Greenwich Village, semble être sorti tout droit de son film préféré «The Awful Truth» (Cette sacrée vérité) avec Irene Dunne et Cary Grant. Avec l'aide de Mark McDonald, directeur de la galerie Fifty/50, Milhaupt a réuni avec charme et humour des meubles et des objets datant des années 30 aux années 60. Il n'accorde guère d'importance aux tapis et aux rideaux et qualifie son style d'antidécoratif. Quand on lui demande s'il a encore un souhait, il répond – bien que sa collection soit déjà digne d'un musée – qu'il aimerait posséder un Picasso. Et pourquoi justement un Picasso? «Afin de pouvoir l'échanger contre une foule d'objets des années 40 et 50.»

Charles M. Milhaupt

Charles M. Milhaupt grew up in California, was trained in the film business, and is now a trustee of the Howard Gilman Foundation, a philanthropic organization. Since his hobby is American films of the 30s and 40s, it is no coincidence that his three-room, 240 sq.m. apartment in a Greenwich Village building from the 30s looks like a movie set from his favorite film "The Awful Truth", starring Irene Dunne and Cary Grant. Assisted by the New York gallery owner Mark McDonald (Fifty/50), Milhaupt has brilliantly put together a charming collection of furniture and objects from the 30s to the 60s. He does not attach much importance to carpets and curtains, calling his style anti-decorative. Asked whether his museum-quality collection lacked anything, Milhaupt replied that a Picasso would be nice. Why a Picasso? So he could trade it for loads of 40s and 50s pieces.

Aufgewachsen in Kalifornien und ausgebildet im Film-Business hat Charles M. Milhaupt – Treuhänder der philanthropischen Howard-Gilman-Stiftung – ein Faible für amerikanische Filme der 30er und 40er Jahre. Und so kommt es nicht von ungefähr, daß sein 240 m² großes Drei-Zimmer-Apartment in einem Gebäude der 30er Jahre in Greenwich Village aussieht, als stamme es aus seinem Lieblingsfilm »The Awful Truth« (Schreckliche Wahrheit) mit Irene Dunne und Cary Grant. Mit Hilfe des New Yorker Galeristen Mark McDonald von Fifty/50 hat Milhaupt Möbel und Objekte aus den 30er bis 60er Jahren mit geradezu genialem Charme und Witz zusammengestellt. Auf Teppiche und Vorhänge legt er nicht viel Wert, und seinen Stil nennt er anti-dekorativ. Auf die Frage, ob er noch einen Wunsch offen habe für seine durchaus museumsreife Sammlung, antwortet er, daß er gern einen Picasso hätte. Warum ausgerechnet einen Picasso? »Damit ich ihn gegen jede Menge Objekte aus den 40er und 50er Jahren eintauschen kann.«

Page de gauche: T.H. Robsjohn-Gibbings a conçu dans les années 40 le canapé gris et les lampes de table. Le tableau est de Rem Kohlhaas; il s'agit d'un croquis que l'architecte hollandais réalisa en 1976/77 pour le Welfare Hotel.

Ci-dessus à gauche: chaise «Wire Cone», 1959, du designer danois Verner Panton, qui vit aujourd'hui en Suisse; petit ensemble de bureau de Charles et Ray Eames, 1950. Pastel de James Ford; vase du dessus: création de Walter Teague pour Steuben, vers 1940. Vase «Mouchoir» de Venini, années 50.

Ci-dessus à droite: sur le meuble bas danois aux tiroirs bombés (ce n'est pas une pièce de designer), un dessin de Keith Haring, 1988, et un portrait de l'écrivain William Somerset Maugham par le photographe George Platt Lynes.

Facing page: The gray sofa and table lamps are T.H. Robsjohn-Gibbings designs from the 40s. The picture is a 1976/77 drawing by the Dutch architect Rem Kohlhaas for the Welfare Hotel.

Above left: "Wire Cone" chair by Danish designer Verner Panton, 1959, who presently lives in Switzerland. The pastel is by James Ford. The small office unit is by Charles and Ray Eames, 1950; the design for the vase above is by Walter Teague for Steuben Glass, and the "handkerchief"-design vase by Venini.

Above right: On the Danish sideboard with wave-fronted drawers – not a designer piece! – a drawing by Keith Haring, 1988, and a portrait of the author William Somerset Maugham by photographer George Platt Lynes, 1941.

Linke Seite: Das graue Sofa und die Tischlampen hat T.H. Robsjohn-Gibbings in den 40er Jahren entworfen. Das Bild ist von Rem Kohlhaas und zeigt einen 1976/77 entstandenen Entwurf des holländischen Architekten für das Welfare Hotel.

Oben links: »Wire-Cone«-Stuhl des heute in der Schweiz lebenden dänischen Designers Verner Panton von 1959. Das Pastell ist von James Ford. Die Fächer des kleinen Büroregals von Charles und Ray Eames von 1950 dekorieren Vasen: die obere wurde von Walter Teague für Steuben entworfen, die »Taschentuch«-Vase stammt von Venini.

Oben rechts: Auf einem dänischen Sideboard mit gewellten Schubladen – kein Designerstück! – stehen eine Zeichnung von Keith Haring von 1988 und eine Fotografie von George Platt Lynes mit dem Porträt des Schriftstellers William Somerset Maugham von 1941.

Ci-dessus: au-dessus du lit, un triptyque des Weimaraner de William Wegman, 1988.
A droite: La cuisine est minuscule mais fonctionnelle. Les stores véni-tiens en lamelles de bois très fines ont été fabriqués sur mesure.
Page de droite: Le canapé-pastilles est deux fois plus large que la ver-sion normale de George Nelson de 1952. Cet exemplaire hors-série a été fabriqué en 1956 par Herman Miller. Au-dessus, «Orion Blanc», tapisserie murale de Victor Vasarely.

Above: Above the bed hangs a tryptich of William Wegman's Weimaraner dogs.
Right: The kitchen is tiny but efficient. The venetian blinds of paper-thin wood are custom-made.
Facing page: The marshmallow sofa by George Nelson, 1952, double the normal size, was custom-made in 1956 for Consolidated Edison's main administrative office. Above it is Victor Vasarely's op art Aubus-son tapestry "Orion Blanc".

Oben: über dem Bett ein Triptychon der Weimaraner Hunde von William Wegman.
Rechts: Die Küche ist winzig, aber praktisch. Die venezianischen Jalousien aus hauchdünnem Holz sind maßgefertigt.
Rechte Seite: Doppelt so breit wie die Normalversion ist dieses Marshmallow-Sofa von George Nelson von 1952, eine Sonderanferti-gung aus dem Jahr 1956 von Herman Miller. Darüber Victor Vasa-relys Aubusson-Wandteppich »Orion Blanc« von 1965.

Contrairement à beaucoup d'artistes new-yorkais, le joaillier-orfèvre
Ted Muehling fait une nette distinction entre son travail et sa vie privée. Sa boutique se trouve au rez-de-chaussée d'un bâtiment d'usine
de SoHo, au 47 Greene Street. Après avoir visité 150 maisons, il a fini
par découvrir l'appartement idéal à Greenwich Village et ce, à même
pas un quart d'heure de marche de son atelier. Grand liseur devant
l'Eternel, Muehling a fait de cet appartement situé dans une rue
calme un refuge qui a énormément de style. Les murs sont peints en
dégradés de vert et de gris des mers du Nord, couleurs des coquillages
et des huîtres dont on retrouve aussi les formes dans ses bijoux et
objets. Les ouvrages de Muehling sont des compositions d'argent et
de verre avec des écailles, des brindilles de nids abandonnés, des
coquillages et des coraux. Il a déjà remporté par deux fois le célèbre
prix Coty du meilleur design. Afin de pouvoir répondre à la demande,
il embauche un employé après l'autre. Avec sa sensibilité d'artisan,
il se refuse à faire entrer chez lui ordinateurs et robots.

Ted Muehling

Unlike many New York artists, silversmith and jewelry designer Ted
Muehling strictly separates his working area from his living area.
His shop and workshop are on the ground floor of a factory building at 47 Greene Street in SoHo. In Greenwich Village, less than a
fifteen-minute walk away, he found an ideal apartment – after
looking at 150 others. The quiet street makes his place the perfect
refuge for an avid reader. The walls are finished in delicate shad-
ings of green and aqua, the colors of seashells and oysters, whose
natural forms recur in his designs. Jewelry and objects by Muehling
are delicate organic compositions of silver and glass, often with
tortoise shell, tiny twigs from abandoned bird's nests, seashells
and coral. He is a twice winner of the renowned Coty Design prize.
To keep up with demand, Muehling constantly hires new em-
ployees, but rejects machine and computer-aided production.

Im Gegensatz zu vielen New Yorker Künstlern trennt der Silber-
schmied und Schmuckdesigner Ted Muehling Arbeiten und Wohnen
strikt. Seine Ladenwerkstatt liegt im Parterre des Fabrikgebäudes Nr.
47 Greene Street in SoHo. Keine fünfzehn Minuten Fußweg entfernt
hat er in einem schmalen Mietshaus in Greenwich Village nach lan-
gem Suchen – 150 Besichtigungen! – ein ideales Apartment gefunden. In einer ruhigen baumbestandenen Straße gelegen ist seine
Wohnung ein stilvolles Refugium für den leidenschaftlichen Leser. Die
Wände sind in zarten Schattierungen von Grün und Meergrau gehalten, den Farben von Muscheln und Austern – Naturformen, die
sich in seinen Designarbeiten wiederfinden. Schmuck und Objekte
von Muehling sind zarte organische Kompositionen aus Silber und
Glas mit Schildpatt, mit Ästchen aus verlassenen Vogelnestern, mit
Muscheln und Korallen. Zweimal wurde er bereits mit dem renommierten Coty-Designpreis ausgezeichnet. Um mit der starken Nach-
frage Schritt zu halten, stellt Muehling einen Mitarbeiter nach dem
anderen ein. Computer und Automaten kommen dem sensiblen
Handwerker allerdings nicht ins Haus.

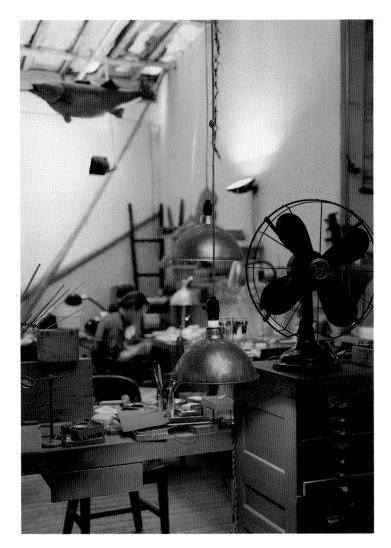

Page précédente: dans l'atelier de Muehling, pas de tableaux au mur mais quelques exemplaires de sa collection de 80 chaises au-dessus de la table à émailler. En haut à gauche, un fauteuil en teck du designer danois Hans Wegner, 1949. Au centre, un fauteuil à bascule en jonc tressé de l'atelier new-yorkais New Lebanon de la secte Amish.
Ci-dessus: le maître au travail. Muehling fait tout à la main, même les croquis qu'il dessine avec un crayon et non pas à l'aide d'un ordinateur.
Page de droite: Le matin, Muehling met un quart d'heure pour aller de son appartement de Greenwich Village à son lieu de travail dans la Green Street à SoHo. Devant, le magasin; derrière, l'atelier. Vitrines et table de Chris Lehrecke, chaise en aluminium des années 50.

Previous page: In Muehling's workshop, above his table for enamel work, some of the eighty chairs in his collection decorate the wall. On the upper left is a classic armchair of teakwood by Danish designer Hans Wegner, 1949, and, second from right, a bullrush-weave rocker from the workshop of the Amish in New Lebanon, New York.
Above: The master at work. Every item is done by hand. His drafting is also done by hand, not by computer.

Facing page: Early every morning, Muehling takes a fifteen-minute walk to work, from his apartment in Greenwich Village to his studio on Greene Street in SoHo. The sales area is in front, the workshop in the rear. The showcases and table are by Chris Lehrecke, the aluminum chair is from the 50s.

Vorhergehende Seite: In der Werkstatt hängen über dem Emailliertisch Exponate aus Muehlings 80 Exemplare umfassender Stuhlsammlung. Links oben ein Armlehnstuhl aus Teakholz des dänischen Designers Hans Wegner von 1949 und in der Mitte ein Schaukelstuhl mit Binsengeflecht aus der New Yorker New-Lebanon-Werkstatt der amerikanischen Amish-Sekte.
Oben: der Meister bei der Arbeit. Alles ist handgearbeitet. Auch seine Entwürfe entstehen mit dem Stift und nicht am Computer.
Rechte Seite: Eine Viertelstunde geht Muehling frühmorgens von seiner Wohnung in Greenwich Village zu seiner Arbeitsstätte in der Greene Street von SoHo, vorne Laden, hinten Werkstatt. Schaukästen und Tisch von Chris Lehrecke, Aluminiumstuhl aus den 50er Jahren.

New York Interiors   Ted Muehling

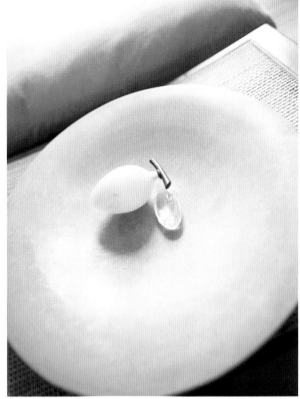

Double page précédente: *Bijoux et œuvres d'art de Ted Muehling qui allie l'argent aux matériaux naturels, comme les coquillages, les coquilles d'œufs, les nids d'oiseaux, etc.*
Ci-dessus: *l'appartement à Greenwich Village, dans un petit immeuble de location de quatre étages. Sur la cheminée, des coquillages, une carapace de tortue et des objets en céramique scandinaves et japonais. Chaises de Paul McCobb, photo de Bill Jacobson; à gauche, petite statue de chaise en bronze de Michele Oka Doner. Appuis-tête africains.*
Page de droite: *au-dessus de la cheminée en briques réfractaires, un os de baleine; sur la table de Chris Gehrecke, des bois d'élan. Les chaises près de la table sont de Paul McCobb, à côté de la cheminée, de Hans Wegner. Fauteuil de T.H. Robsjohn-Gibbings, plafonnier d'Ingo Maurer.*

Previous pages: *jewelry and art objects by Ted Muehling. He combines silver with materials from nature, such as seashells, egg shells, and bird's nests.*
Above: *the apartment in Greenwich Village, in a narrow four-storey building. On the mantel seashells, tortoiseshells and Scandinavian and Japanese ceramics. The chairs are by Paul McCobb, the photo by Bill Jacobson, the small bronze chair sculpture left of the fireplace is by Michèle Oka Doner. The headrests are from Africa.*

Facing page: *on the mantel of the brick fireplace a whalebone, on the dining room table by Chris Gehrecke an elk's antlers. The chairs are by Paul McCobb, the easy chair by T.H. Robsjohn-Gibbings, the chairs beside the fireplace by Hans Wegner. The ceiling lamp is by Ingo Maurer.*

Vorhergehende Doppelseite: *Schmuck und Kunst von Ted Muehling, der Silber mit Materialien aus der Natur verbindet, beispielsweise Muscheln, Eierschalen oder Vogelnestern.*
Oben: *das Apartment in Greenwich Village in einem schmalen vierstöckigen Mietshaus. Auf dem Kaminsims Muscheln, ein Schildkrötenpanzer sowie skandinavische und japanische Keramik. Die Stühle stammen von Paul McCobb, das Foto ist von Bill Jacobson. Vor dem Kamin eine kleine Bronzestuhl-Plastik von Michèle Oka Doner und Kopfstützen aus Afrika.*
Rechte Seite: *über dem Schamottkamin ein Walfischknochen und auf dem Eßtisch von Chris Gehrecke ein Elchgeweih. Die Stühle am Tisch sind von Paul McCobb, die neben dem Kamin von Hans Wegner. Der Sessel wurde von T.H. Robsjohn-Gibbings angefertigt, die Deckenlampe von Ingo Maurer.*

Muehling quitte rarement New York, mais s'évade par la lecture. La récamière de T.H. Robsjohn-Gibbings invite au repos. A droite, à côté de l'armoire, une chaise Thonet, les appuis-tête africains font office de repose-pieds.

Muehling rarely leaves New York, but books provide imaginary journeys, especially while resting on the daybed by T.H. Robsjohn-Gibbings. On the right, beside the closet is a Thonet chair, African headrests function as footstools.

Muehling verläßt New York selten – seine Reisen finden beim Lesen statt, im Kopf. Einen Platz zum Ausruhen bietet die Récamiere von T.H. Robsjohn-Gibbings. Rechts neben dem Schrank ein Thonet-Stuhl, Kopfstützen aus Afrika dienen als Fußbank.

New York Interiors   Ted Muehling

Séparée de la salle de séjour par une porte coulissante, la chambre à coucher est la seule pièce dépouillée. Ce qui ressemble à une installation est en fait sa penderie. Suspendus à sept crochets dans le style shaker, chemise, veste, pantalon, etc. pour les sept jours de la semaine. Des valises chinoises empilées les unes sur les autres constituent la table de nuit. La Lampe provient d'un marché aux puces.

The bedroom, separated from the living room by a sliding door, is the only bare room in Muehling's life. What looks like an installation is actually his closet. Seven hooks hold shirts, jackets and pants for the seven days of the week. The night table is a tower of Chinese suitcases, the lamp is from the fleamarket.

Das Schlafzimmer, das durch eine Schiebetür vom Wohnzimmer getrennt wird, ist der einzige karge Raum in Muehlings Wohnung. Was wie eine Installation aussieht, ist in Wirklichkeit seine Garderobe. An sieben Haken hängen im Shaker-Stil Hemd, Jacke, Hose für die sieben Tage der Woche. Der Nachttisch ist ein Turm aus chinesischen Koffern. Die Lampe stammt vom Flohmarkt.

Pendant trois ans Paul F. Ochs III, décorateur, et Osvaldo Gomariz,
peintre et médecin né en Argentine, ont travaillé à la restauration de
l'entrepôt de l'American Beverage Company à Brooklyn. Construit en
1860, le bâtiment était complètement délabré. Peu de temps après
la remise en état, l'artiste mourut prématurément à l'âge de 44 ans.
Arrivé à New York au début des années 70 avec une bourse du Guggenheim, Gomariz avait donné l'exemple à de nombreux artistes en
quittant Greenwich Village de plus en plus envahi par les touristes
pour s'installer à Brooklyn. Il avait fondé une colonie d'artistes dans
le haut bâtiment de briques de la Berry Street. Aujourd'hui, des
peintres, sculpteurs et designers amis travaillent dans le vaste atelier
réparti sur trois étages. Et chacun d'eux a contribué à la décoration
du loft de Gomariz. Un designer a fabriqué l'armoire encastrée, un
sculpteur les montants en fer pour le lit à baldaquin, un autre les
plaques en granit de la cuisine intégrée.

Paul F. Ochs III

Interior designer Paul F. Ochs III and Argentine-born Osvaldo
Gomariz, painter and physician, worked for three years on the
restoration of their dilapidated Brooklyn warehouse. Built in 1860,
it was once owned by the American Beverage Company. Not long
after their work was done, the artist died prematurely, at forty-four.
Gomariz had come to New York in the early 70s on a Guggenheim
Fellowship. He was a pioneer in the move of many artists to
Brooklyn, away from Greenwich Village and its throngs of tourists.
He founded an artist's colony in the high brick building on Berry
Street. Today his friends – painters, sculptors and designers – work
in the spacious studios on three floors. And each one has con-
tributed his share in refurbishing the Gomariz loft. A designer in-
stalled the built-in closets, a sculptor devised the iron posts for the
canopy on the bed, another made the granite slabs in the kitchen.

Drei Jahre lang haben der Interior-Designer Paul F. Ochs III und der
in Argentinien geborene Maler und Arzt Osvaldo Gomariz an der Restaurierung des 1860 erbauten, verfallenen Lagerhauses der American
Beverage Company in Brooklyn gearbeitet. Kurz darauf verstarb der
Künstler viel zu früh – mit 44 Jahren. Gomariz, der mit einem Gug-
genheim-Stipendium Anfang der 70er Jahre nach New York kam,
initiierte den Rückzug vieler Künstler aus dem immer touristischeren
Greenwich Village nach Brooklyn. In dem hohen Backsteingebäude
an der Berry Street hatte er eine Künstlerkolonie gegründet. Heute
arbeiten in den großzügigen, auf drei Stockwerke verteilten Ateliers
befreundete Maler, Bildhauer und Designer. Und jeder hat seinen
Teil zur Gestaltung des Gomariz-Lofts beigetragen. Ein Designer
fertigte die Schrankeinbauten, ein Bildhauer die Eisenpfosten für das
Himmelbett, ein anderer die Granitplatten der Küchenzeile.

Page précédente: De la terrasse du toit de l'ancient entrepôt de Brooklyn, entre Williamsburg et Greenpoint, on peut voir tout Manhattan, de Wallstreet Downtown à la 100th Street de Upper Manhattan. La fenêtre au-dessus de l'évier donne sur le World Trade Center.
Ci-dessus: La table de bistro de 4 m de long invite à déjeuner et à lire le journal.

Previous page: From the roof terrace of the former warehouse in Brooklyn, between Williamsburg and Greenpoint, the entire sweep of Manhattan can be seen, from downtown Wall Street to 100th Street in uptown Manhattan. The towers of the World Trade Center are visible through the kitchen window.
Above: The more than 4 m long bistro table is an invitation to have a leisurely meal over the newspaper.

Vorhergehende Seite: Von der Dachterrasse des ehemaligen Lagerhauses in Brooklyn zwischen Williamsburg und Greenpoint überblickt man ganz Manhattan von der Wallstreet Downtown bis zur 100th Street in Upper Manhattan. Durch das Fenster über dem Spülbecken zeichnet sich das World Trade Center ab.
Oben: Der 4 m lange Bistrotisch lädt ein zum Zeitunglesen und Essen.

Une estrade en bois délimite la partie atelier de la partie logement du peintre. Avec ses dix-huit fenêtres, le loft du dernier étage de l'American Beverage offre une vue circulaire sur Brooklyn jusqu'à Manhattan.

A wooden platform raises the painter's living area above the working area. With eighteen windows, the top-floor loft of the American Beverage Building offers an unobstructed panoramic view across Brooklyn to Manhattan.

Ein Holzpodest hebt den Wohn- über den Arbeitsbereich des Malers. Der Loft im obersten Stock des American-Beverage-Gebäudes bietet mit achtzehn Fenstern einen Rundblick über Brooklyn bis nach Manhattan.

New York Interiors   Paul F. Ochs III

Double page précédente: Haut de 5 m, le plafond a conservé son état primitif, y compris les conduits et les poutres non poncées. Au centre de la pièce, le toit vitré offre au peintre les meilleures conditions de travail. A gauche, sur l'estrade, le coin cuisine/salle à manger; à droite, le sol de l'atelier est en asphalte. Accrochés sur le mur du fond, des tableaux de Gomariz.
Page de gauche: C'est en achetant la «Guitar Chair» en métal de l'artiste new-yorkais Linus Coraggio que Gomariz rencontra le décorateur Paul F. Ochs III. Plus tard, il lui demanda de l'aider à aménager son loft. Le tableau est de Gomariz.
Ci-dessus: Drapée autour de montants en acier, une volumineuse tente en mousseline forme un ciel de lit clair et frais. Le coin chambre est contigu au séjour sur l'estrade. A gauche, les conduites d'eau hors service font l'effet de sculptures.

Previous pages: The 5 m high ceiling was left in its original state with pipes exposed and beams unfinished. The large ceiling lamp in the center provides optimal lighting for the painter. Left, on the platform, is the cooking/eating area. The studio, on the right, has an asphalt floor. On the front wall are pictures by Gomariz.
Facing page: On the occasion of his purchase of the metal "Guitar Chair" by New York artist Linus Coraggio, Gomariz met interior designer Paul F. Ochs III, whom he subsequently asked to help furnish his loft. The picture is by Gomariz.
Above: An opulent tent of muslin is draped over steel pipes to form a canopy over the big bed. Sleeping and adjacent living areas lie on the raised wooden floor. The disconnected water pipes, left, have the look of sculptures.

Vorhergehende Doppelseite: 5 m hoch ist die Decke, die im Originalzustand belassen wurde – inklusive Leitungen und rohe Balken. In der Mitte spendet ein großes Oberlicht dem Maler beste Arbeitsbedingungen. Links auf dem Podest der Koch- und Eßbereich, rechts auf Asphalt das Atelier. An der Frontwand ein Gemälde von Gomariz.
Linke Seite: Beim Kauf des metallenen »Guitar-Chair« des New Yorker Künstlers Linus Coraggio lernte Gomariz den Interior-Designer Paul F. Ochs III kennen. Später bat er ihn um Hilfe bei der Einrichtung des Lofts. Das Gemälde ist von Gomariz.
Oben: Ein opulentes Zelt aus Musselintüchern, die über dem großen Bett um Stahlrohre drapiert wurden, bildet einen heiteren Betthimmel. Der Schlafbereich schließt sich auf dem Holzpodest an den Wohnbereich an. Die stillgelegten Wasserrohre links wirken wie Skulpturen.

Voici quinze ans que Michele Oka Doner a débarqué à New York
avec son mari, ses fils et ses perroquets. Après avoir grandi dans les
vastes étendues du Middle West, elle a vécu sur les plages de Miami.
Et maintenant, la voilà dans la fièvre new-yorkaise. Aujourd'hui, elle
a l'impression d'avoir toujours habité cette ville. Situé dans le quartier
artistique de SoHo, son imposant loft de la Mercer Street était autrefois une fabrique de bonbons construite en 1880. Il lui sert à la fois
d'atelier, de salle d'exposition et d'appartement. Oka Doner affirme
qu'à l'instar des anciennes cultures, elle a organisé sa vie et son travail autour d'un foyer imaginaire. Une belle image pour ce loft lumineux dont les hautes fenêtres font entrer énormément de clarté. Ses
créations sont éparpillées partout et se mêlent à des objets trouvés
dans la nature; sur les consoles et dans les niches, on découvre sa
collection de déesses précolombiennes de la fécondité. Oka Doner les
trouve particulièrement inspirantes.

Michèle Oka Doner

Fifteen years ago, designer and sculptress Michèle Oka Doner
arrived in New York with husband, sons and parrots. She had
grown up in Miami, after a Midwestern childhood. Now Oka Doner
cannot imagine ever not having lived in frenetic New York. Her im-
pressive loft, on Mercer Street in the creative SoHo area, was built
in 1880 as a candy factory. It is workshop, showroom and domicile
in one. She says that she structured her life and her work around
an imaginary fireplace, as in ancient cultures. It is an apt image for
the brightly lit loft, where the sun shines profusely through high
windows, unusual for New York. Prototypes and models by the designer are standing, leaning, lying around everywhere, interspersed
with natural objects and, on brackets and in niches, her collection
of pre-Columbian fertility goddesses, which she finds especially
inspiring.

Vor fünfzehn Jahren kam die Designerin und Bildhauerin Michèle
Oka Doner mit Mann, Söhnen und Papageien nach New York. Aufgewachsen am Strand von Miami, hatte sie vorher im weiten Mittle-
ren Westen Amerikas gelebt. Und nun die fiebernde Stadt New York.
Heute kann sich Oka Doner nicht vorstellen, jemals nicht hier gelebt
zu haben. Ihr imposanter Loft, der 1880 als Bonbonfabrik erbaut
wurde und in der Mercer Street im Kreativen-Viertel SoHo liegt, ist
Werkstatt, Showroom und Wohnung in einem. Ihr Leben und ihre
Arbeit hat sie – wie in alten Kulturen – um eine imaginäre Feuerstelle
angelegt. Ein schönes Bild für den hellen Loft, durch dessen hohe Fenster für New Yorker Verhältnisse geradezu verschwenderisch die Sonne
scheint – wenn sie scheint. Überall liegen, stehen, lehnen Entwürfe
der Designerin, und dazwischen ruhen Fundstücke aus der Natur. Auf
Konsolen und in Nischen ist ihre Sammlung präkolumbianischer
Fruchtbarkeitsgöttinnen untergebracht, die sie besonders inspirierend
findet.

Première page: *La bibliothèque constitue le cœur du loft. Composée d'étagères préfabriquées, elle est l'œuvre d'Erich Theophile, architecte de Boston. Theophile s'y connaît en pièces particulièrement hautes (celle-ci fait 6 m), ayant restauré entre autres le palais royal de Katmandou. Contre la colonne, une chaise en bronze Web/Coral de Michèle Oka Doner.*

Double page précédente: *vue depuis la galerie sur la salle de travail et le séjour avec les énormes bancs «Ice-Ring». Sur le piano à queue, des moules d'Oka Doner. Anciens radiateurs en fer autour des colonnes.*

Ci-dessus: *modèles réduits des chaises en bronze doré d'Oka Doner sur le banc circulaire; au fond, la galerie.*

Page de droite: *La vaste cour ensoleillée éclaire le coin cuisine/repas. La lourde table en marbre noir est une création d'Oka Doner.*

First page: *The heart of the loft is a library, conceived by Erich Theophile, an architect from Boston, using prefabricated shelves. Theophile has a good eye for the height of a room, which in this case is almost 6 m high. One of his assignments was the restoration of the Royal Nepalese palaces of Katmandu. Leaning against the column is a bronze fan coral chair by Michèle Oka Doner.*

Previous pages: *view from the gallery down into the living room/studio of the designer with her giant "Ice-Ring" benches. On the grand piano casting molds by Oka Doner. Antique cast-iron radiators surround the base of the columns.*

Above: *gilded mini-models of Oka Doner's bronze chairs on the ring bench, with the gallery in the background.*

Facing page: *From the spacious interior court sun falls into the kitchen/eating area. The massive table of black French marble is an Oka Doner design.*

Erste Seite: *Das Herzstück des Lofts ist eine Bibliothek, die von Erich Theophile, einem Architekten aus Boston, aus vorgefertigten Regalen zusammengestellt wurde. Theophile hat ein gutes Gefühl für Raumhöhe, die hier 6 m mißt. Er restaurierte unter anderem die königlich-nepalesischen Paläste von Katmandu. An der Säule lehnt ein bronzener Webkorallen-Stuhl von Michèle Oka Doner.*

Vorhergehende Doppelseite: *Blick von der Galerie in den Wohn- und Arbeitsraum der Designerin mit ihren riesigen »Ice-Ring«-Bänken. Auf dem Flügel liegen Gußformen von Oka Doner. Um die Säulen alte Heizkörper aus Eisen.*

Oben: *vergoldete Mini-Modelle von Oka Doners Bronzestühlen auf der »Ice-Ring«-Bank, im Hintergrund die Galerie.*

Rechte Seite: *Aus dem weiten Innenhof fallen Sonnenstrahlen in den Küchen- und Eßbereich. Der schwere Tisch aus schwarzem französischen Marmor ist ein Entwurf von Oka Doner.*

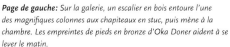

Page de gauche: Sur la galerie, un escalier en bois entoure l'une des magnifiques colonnes aux chapiteaux en stuc, puis mène à la chambre. Les empreintes de pieds en bronze d'Oka Doner aident à se lever le matin.

Ci-dessus: Une galerie coudée sépare en deux étages le loft de 1550 m². Les intéressantes constructions d'escaliers conduisent à la chambre et à la salle de bains. L'étage inférieur est réservé au séjour et aux salles de travail. On passe indifféremment des pièces à usage privé aux pièces officielles. Seul l'atelier avec son poêle s'est vu attribuer une pièce séparée sous la galerie.

Facing page: Above, on the gallery, a wooden staircase skirts one of the magnificent columns with their stuccoed capitals and leads into the bedroom. Oka Doner's bronze footprints help her start the day on the right track.

Above: The large, almost 1550 sq.m. loft area is divided into two levels by a sweeping gallery. The intriguing stair constructions lead up into the bed- and bathrooms. The lower level comprises living and work rooms, providing a natural flow between diversified private and official functions. Only the workshop containing the kiln is in a separate room below the gallery.

Linke Seite: Oben auf der Galerie führt eine Holztreppe um eine der prunkvollen Säulen mit Stuckkapitell ins Schlafzimmer. Oka Doners Fußabdrücke aus Bronze erleichtern das Aufstehen.

Oben: Der 1550 m² große Loftraum wird durch eine geschwungene Galerie in zwei Etagen geteilt. Interessante Treppenkonstruktionen führen nach oben in die Schlaf- und Badezimmer. Auf der unteren Ebene befinden sich Wohn- und Arbeitsräume. Die privaten und offiziellen Raumfunktionen fließen ineinander über. Nur die Werkstatt mit dem Brennofen hat unter der Galerie einen separaten Raum erhalten.

Sa mode est spectaculaire et ludique. Star des grands couturiers, le New-Yorkais Todd Oldham affirme qu'il entreprend tout dans la vie avec les yeux d'un gamin de 13 ans. C'est à cet âge que la grande aventure de sa vie a commencé. Dans un fastfood de Denver, il fut témoin d'un hold-up et n'en sortit indemne qu'en allant se cacher dans un réfrigérateur. Depuis, il ne veut voir que le côté cocasse des choses. Et il semble s'être bien amusé avec son partenaire Tony Longoria quand ils ont aménagé son appartement de Manhattan. Celui-ci est un temple du kitch, les objets ayant été découverts sur les marchés aux puces des environs. Les seules choses qui ont de la valeur sont les tableaux d'Ellen Berkenbilt et les photos de Diane Arbus, Cindy Sherman, Lee Friedlander et quelques autres. Parfois, le tapis en sisal du salon donne lieu à des élans créatifs. Car chaque fois que Betty et Mike, les turbulents terriers de Todd, s'oublient sur le tapis, Oldham repeint les taches personnellement. La vie est un jeu.

Todd Oldham

His fashions are spectacular and playful. Star New York fashion designer Todd Oldham says candidly that he approaches everything in life with the mentality of a thirteen-year-old. That was his age when the adventure of his life began. He survived a violent holdup in a fast-food place in Denver only because he managed to hide in the refrigerator. From then on his main objective has been to have fun. Obviously he and his partner Tony Longoria had plenty when they made their Manhattan apartment a temple of pure kitsch, discovered at nearby fleamarkets. The only really valuable items are paintings by Ellen Berkenbilt and photographs by Diane Arbus, Cindy Sherman and Lee Friedlander, among others. The sisal carpet in the living room becomes the object of animal creativity at times, when Betty and Mike, Todd's wild terriers soil the rug. Then Oldham personally paints over the spots. Life is a cabaret…

Seine Mode ist spektakulär und spielerisch. Der New Yorker Mode-design-Star Todd Oldham behauptet von sich schlicht und einfach, daß er alles im Leben mit der Psyche eines 13jährigen Jungen angehe. So alt war er nämlich, als sich das größte Abenteuer seines Lebens ereignete: Einen Überfall auf einen Fastfood-Laden in Denver überlebte er nur deshalb unverletzt, weil er sich vor den schwerbewaffneten Gangstern in einem Kühlschrank versteckte. Spaß ist seitdem oberste Pflicht. Jede Menge davon hatten er und sein Partner Tony Longoria ganz offensichtlich, als sie ihr Apartment in Manhattan einrichteten. Es ist ein Tempel für Kitsch, der auf nahen Flohmärkten erworben wurde. Die einzigen wertvollen Stücke sind Gemälde von Ellen Berkenbilt und Arbeiten von Diane Arbus, Cindy Sherman, Lee Friedlander und anderen Fotografen. Tierische Kreativität entfaltet sich manchmal auf einem hellen Sisalteppich im Salon: Immer wenn Betty und Mike, Todds wilde Terrier, mal wieder nicht ganz sauber waren, übermalt Oldham persönlich die zurückgebliebenen Flecken. Alles im Leben ist ein Spiel.

Page précédente: l'autel domestique d'Oldham. La photo de gauche est de Diane Arbus, celle de droite de Leon Borensztein. La nature morte aux fleurs provient du marché aux puces. Portrait de Todd Oldham par Dan Rizzie sur la photo de détail.

Page de gauche: Recouvert d'une mosaïque Memory, le meuble Entertainment dissimule un énorme téléviseur. Le tapis à rayures arc-en-ciel est une fabrication hors série.

Ci-dessus: Betty et Mike, les terriers Black and White d'Oldham, sont assis dans le salon entre les deux canapés recouverts d'un damas de soie bleue façon Empire. Le mur est le «Wall of Women»; tous les portraits de femmes ont été achetés au marché aux puces.

Pages suivantes, de gauche à droite et de haut en bas: un arrangement de roses en soie sur un fauteuil; une veste de paillettes avec le portrait du terrier Mike; une assiette-souvenir avec le président Lyndon et sa femme, sur une couverture patchwork aux drapeaux internationaux; devant le tableau d'Ellen Berkenbilt, une collection disparate d'oiseaux du marché aux puces et devant, des énormes bijoux en verre.

Pages suivantes à droite: dans le coin salle à manger, des petites huiles d'Ellen Berkenbilt autour d'une lampe funèbre de Godley-Schwan. Des animaux fantastiques sont tapis sur des tabourets africains et américains.

Previous pages: Oldham's altar. The photo on the left is by Diane Arbus, that on the right by Leon Borensztein. The flower still life hails from the fleamarket. The portrait of Todd Oldham is by Dan Rizzie.

Facing page: The entertainment console, concealing a giant television set, is covered with a mosaic of memo stickers. The brilliantly striped carpet with the colors of the rainbow was custom-made.

Above: In the salon, two Empire-style sofas are covered in silk-damask fabric. Between the sofas, on a Lamontage carpet, Oldham's black and white terriers, Betty and Mike, sit to attention. All the portraits on the "Wall of Women" were acquired at fleamarkets.

Following pages left, clockwise from top left: a chair with an arrangement of silk roses; a sequined jacket with a portrait of Mike the terrier; a souvenir plate depicting President Lyndon B. Johnson and his wife Lady Bird, on a patchwork cover with international flags. In front of the picture by Ellen Berkenbilt, a congeries of birds from the fleamarket, in front, gigantic glass gems.

Following pages, right: In the dining area small oil paintings by Ellen Berkenbilt frame a totem lamp by Godley-Schwan. Little fantastic animals are lurking on African and American stools.

Vorhergehende Seiten: Oldhams Hausaltar. Das linke Foto ist von Diane Arbus, das rechte von Leon Borensztein. Blumenstilleben vom Flohmarkt. Das Detailfoto zeigt Todd Oldham, porträtiert von Dan Rizzie.

Linke Seite: Das Entertainment-Möbel ist mit einem Memory-Mosaik beklebt und verbirgt einen riesigen Fernseher. Der in kräftigen Regenbogenfarben gestreifte Teppich ist eine Sonderanfertigung.

Oben: Oldhams Terrier Betty und Mike stehen im Salon stramm. Mit blauem Seidendamast bezogene Empire-ähnliche Sofas. Die Wand ist die »Wall of Women«: Alle Frauen-Porträts sind von Flohmärkten.

Folgende Seiten links, im Uhrzeigersinn von links oben: Seidenrosen-Arrangement auf Sessel; eine Paillettenjacke mit dem Porträt von Terrier Mike; auf einer Patchworkdecke aus Flaggen ein Souvenierteller mit den Porträts des amerikanischen Präsidenten Lyndon Johnson und First Lady Bird Johnson; vor dem Gemälde von Ellen Berkenbilt ein Vogel-Sammelsurium vom Flohmarkt, davor riesige Glasjuwelen.

Folgende Seiten rechts: Im Eßbereich umrahmen kleine Ölgemälde von Ellen Berkenbilt eine Totemlampe von Godley-Schwan. Auf afrikanischen und amerikanischen Hockern lauern Phantasietierchen.

Chez lui au kibboutz, Izhar Patkin a agrandi sa petite maison de pierre en y ajoutant une tente de bédouin aux dimensions surprenantes. L'artiste israélien, arrivé en Amérique en 1979, a toujours eu besoin d'espace. La première fois qu'il est entré dans le grand bâtiment vide, une ancienne usine de colliers de chien, il a tout de suite senti qu'il avait enfin trouvé ce qu'il lui fallait. L'atmosphère plutôt louche convenait fort bien à cet homme plein d'imagination. Des tas d'affiches représentant des caniches ornaient les murs, des perles, du strass et des factures jonchaient le sol. Au cours d'une orgie de peinture, Patkin et ses amis artistes ont transformé le tout en un habitat riche en couleurs. Patkin vit dans la Lower East Side de Manhattan, un quartier grouillant de vie. Les pleurs des mazurkas s'échappent des fenêtres et se marient au rock heavy-metal. C'est tout à fait dans les goûts d'Izhar Patkin, voyageur curieux qui déambule entre sa terre natale millénaire et son nouvel univers new-yorkais.

Izhar Patkin

During his kibbutz days, Izhar Patkin had enlarged his tiny stone house by adding an enormous Bedouin tent. The Israeli artist, at home in New York since 1979, had always needed a lot of space. As soon as he entered the abandoned dog-collar factory, Patkin knew he had finally found what he was looking for. The artist was enchanted with its bizarre atmosphere: walls covered with posters of poodles, the floor strewn with beads, rhinestones and bills. Patkin and his artist friends threw a wild painting party and transformed it all into a friendly, colorful living space. Patkin lives on Manhattan's Lower East Side, a lively multicultural area with Puerto Rican restaurants, Italian bakeries and kosher delicatessens. The air is pervaded by mazurka laments, punctuated by heavy metal guitars and drums. This is an area Izhar Patkin enjoys, an inquisitive traveller who moves between his ancient homeland and his new New York world.

Im heimischen Kibbuz baute er eines Tages an sein kleines Steinhaus ein überdimensionales Beduinenzelt an. Der israelische Künstler Izhar Patkin, der 1979 nach Amerika kam, brauchte schon immer viel Platz. Als er die große leerstehende Hundehalsband-Fabrik zum ersten Mal betrat, ahnte er, daß er endlich das Passende gefunden hatte. Die schräge Atmosphäre kam dem phantasievollen Mann sehr entgegen: an den Wänden hingen Pudelposter, auf dem Boden lagen Perlen, Straß und Rechnungen. In einer Malorgie verwandelten Patkin und seine Künstlerfreunde das Ganze in einen farbenfrohen Lebensraum. Patkin lebt in der Lower East Side von Manhattan, einem lebhaften multikulturellen Viertel mit puertoricanischen Restaurants, italienischen Bäckereien, und koscheren Delikatessengeschäften. Die Mazurka weint aus den Fenstern und vermählt sich mit Heavy metal. Eine Gegend nach Izhar Patkins Geschmack, dem neugierigen Wanderer zwischen der Jahrtausende alten Heimat und der neuen New Yorker Welt.

New York Interiors   Izhar Patkin

Premières pages: La mini-cuisine est pour ainsi dire engloutie par une peinture murale «Flower Power» de Joey Horatio. La frise est de Patkin: des poules courent le long des murs et se poursuivent autour du vieux flipper. Le tableau est de Richard Phillips.
Pages précédentes, à gauche: Juste à côté de l'entrée du loft, un tableau de Patkin voisinant avec deux tableaux de Nam June Paik. Le collage à droite et la chaise peinte sont de Kim MacConnel.
Pages précédentes, à droite: Le sol du loft est un immense tableau. La statue est de Patkin et Paik.
Ci-dessus: Sur le bureau, une lampe achetée aux Puces côtoie des souvenirs d'Inde, de Grèce et du Mexique. A côté, un robot de Nam June Paik. Au mur jouxtant le lit sont suspendus un tableau de Jean-Michel Basquiat et une peinture de Patkin de sa série «The Five Senses», 1991.
Page de droite: L'image arrêtée sur l'écran de télévision montre un Bouddha la tête en bas. La Table vidéo-plus-œuvre d'art totale est une réalisation commune de Patkin et de Paik. Le rideau en caoutchouc peint est de Patkin.

First pages: A "Flower Power" wall painting by Joey Horatio virtually consumes the tiny kitchen. Patkin's own mural features chicks running along the blue divider and around the vintage pinball machine. The painting is by Richard Phillips.
Previous pages, left: Beside the loft entrance is an image by Patkin, close by are two pictures by Nam June Paik, the collage on the extreme right and the painted chair are by Kim MacConnel.
Previous pages, right: The floor of the loft is a giant carpet painting. The statue is by Patkin and Paik.

Above: On the desk are a lamp from the fleamarket and souvenirs from India, Greece and Mexico, and beside it, a robot by Nam June Paik. On the wall hang a Jean-Michel Basquiat and a Patkin picture from his series "The Five Senses", 1991.
Facing page: Frozen on the television screen is a Buddha, standing on his head. The video-plus-table composition is a Patkin and Paik co-production. The painted rubber curtain is by Patkin.

Erste Seiten: Die winzige Küche wird von einem »Flower Power«-Wandgemälde von Joey Horatio geradezu verschlungen. Auf dem Detailfoto ist ein Wandgemälde von Patkin zu sehen: Hühnchen laufen auf dem blauen Absatz und um den alten Flipperautomaten herum. Das Gemälde ist von Richard Phillips.
Vorhergehende Seiten links: gleich neben dem Lofteingang ein Gemälde von Patkin, daneben zwei Bilder von Nam June Paik. Die Collage rechts außen und der bemalte Stuhl sind von Kim MacConnel.
Vorhergehende Seiten rechts: Den Boden des Lofts bedeckt ein riesiges Teppichgemälde. Die Statue ist von Patkin und Paik.
Oben: auf dem Schreibtisch eine Lampe vom Flohmarkt mit Souvenirs aus Indien, Griechenland und Mexiko. Daneben ein Roboter von Nam June Paik. An der Wand am Bett ein Jean-Michel Basquiat und ein Patkin-Gemälde aus der Serie »The Five Senses« von 1991.
Rechte Seite: Im Fernseher ist ein kopfstehender Buddha eingefroren. Das Video-plus-Tisch-Gesamtkunstwerk ist eine Zusammenarbeit von Patkin und Paik. Den Gummi-Vorhang bemalte Patkin.

Tom et Linda Platt sont mariés depuis vingt-trois ans et parfaitement adaptés l'un à l'autre. Ces stylistes de mode de Midtown Manhattan, dont l'atelier se trouve dans la West 39th Street, habitent dans un immeuble de la Park Avenue, édifié en 1924. Leur nouvel appartement devait avoir la fraîcheur d'une belle journée de printemps. Les architectes contactés, Peter Stamberg et Paul Aferiat, estiment quant à eux que les citadins ont besoin de verdure. Partageant la passion des Platt pour les couleurs vives, ils ont été ravis de pouvoir enfin laisser libre cours à leurs désirs et de jouer avec le vert vénéneux, le rose criard et l'orange flamboyant. Pour les stylistes, cet intérieur aux couleurs franchement osées n'est rien moins que le prolongement de leur conception de la mode. Ce qui est un véritable délice pour les habitants est un choc pour le visiteur non-initié. Mais pour celui qui séjourne ici plus longuement, les couleurs passent à l'arrière-plan et leur effet n'est effectivement plus que tonifiant.

Linda and Tom Platt

Tom and Linda Platt have been married for twenty-three years and they communicate beautifully. Fashion designers from Midtown Manhattan, their studio is on West 39th Street, and they live on Park Avenue in an apartment house that dates to 1924. Their new apartment was meant to have all the freshness of a spring day. Their architects Peter Stamberg and Paul Aferiat agreed, and sharing the Platts' passion for strong colors, they were overjoyed at being able to indulge for once. Greens must be strident. Pinks must scream. Oranges must be bursting with energy. For the designers, the daring color combinations at home are no more and no less than a continuation of their concept of fashion. What may be a feast for the residents' eyes is at first glance a shock for visitors. After a while, however, the colors recede, and their effect becomes merely invigorating.

Seit 23 Jahren sind Tom und Linda Platt verheiratet und mittlerweile perfekt aufeinander abgestimmt. Die Modedesigner aus Midtown Manhattan – ihr Atelier liegt in der West 39th Street – wohnen in der Park Avenue in einem Apartmenthaus aus dem Jahr 1924. Ihre neue Wohnung sollte wie der frischeste Frühlingstag sein. Menschen in der Stadt brauchen ein bißchen Grün – das war auch die Devise der Architekten Peter Stamberg und Paul Aferiat. Sie teilten die Leidenschaft der Platts für kräftige Farben und waren überglücklich, daß sie sich ihrem Farbrausch endlich einmal hemmungslos hingeben konnten. Grün muß giftig sein, Pink muß schreien, Orange vor Kraft strotzen. Für die Designer sind die gewagten Farbkompositionen zu Hause nicht mehr und nicht weniger als eine Fortsetzung ihrer Auffassung von Mode. Was für die Bewohner ein wahrer Augenschmaus ist, wirkt auf Besucher auf den ersten Blick schockierend. Wenn man sich aber länger in der Wohnung aufhält, treten die Farben zurück, und die Wirkung ist tatsächlich nur noch anregend.

Pages précédentes: *des couleurs franches pour un appartement des années 20 dans le style des années 50. Un vert acide et brillant s'étale sur les murs du couloir qui mène au salon. Dans la niche, une Vénus de Milo en plâtre bleu d'Yves Klein. Sur la photo de détail, on voit un groupe de mini-mannequins de confection élevés au rang d'œuvre d'art devant un lourd rideau de taffetas.*

Page de gauche et ci-dessus: *Dans le salon criard, un concert de couleurs discordantes. Citron et herbe fraîche sur les murs, rideaux orange, canapé fuchsia Dialogica de Soho. Les fauteuils des années 50 sont habillés d'une imitation poulain, les sculptures lumineuses sont de Noguchi, le coussin cylindrique est un ballot d'étoffe à paillettes. Seul point reposant pour l'œil: la cheminée noire.*

Previous pages: *strong colors in the style of the 50s for an apartment from the 20s. Bright green lacquer colors the walls in the corridor leading into the living room. In the niche is a blue plaster Venus de Milo by Yves Klein. The detail photo shows artful miniature tailor's dummies before a voluminous taffeta curtain.*

Facing page and above: *The living room is where dazzling colors meet. The walls are lemon and grass-green, the curtains are orange, the sofa by Dialogica of SoHo is pink. The 50s armchair is covered with imitation foalskin, the light sculptures are by Noguchi, the round pillow gleams with sequins. The black fireplace provides an eye-relaxing contrast.*

Vorhergehende Seiten: *starke Farben für ein 20er-Jahre-Apartment im 50er-Jahre-Stil. Giftgrün lackiert sind die Wände im Flur, der in das Wohnzimmer übergeht. In der Nische eine Yves-Klein-blaue Venus von Milo aus Gips. Das Detailfoto zeigt zur Kunst erhobene Miniatur-Anziehpuppen vor einem voluminösen Taftvorhang.*

Linke Seite und oben: *im schrillen Wohnzimmer ein Rendezvous der knalligen Farben. In Zitronengelb und Grasgrün sind die Wände gehalten, in Orange die Vorhänge, in Pink das Sofa von Dialogica in SoHo. Die 50er-Jahre-Sessel sind mit Fohlenfell-Imitat bezogen. Die Lichtskulpturen stammen von Noguchi, die Schlummerrolle ist mit Paillettenstoff bezogen. Ruhepunkt fürs Auge bietet allein der schwarze Kamin.*

Ci-dessus et page de droite: dans la chambre à coucher garde-robe, des modèles de Tom et Linda Platt. Tom Platt a brodé lui-même les coussins jaunes et plissé le couvre-lit de velours. Linda Platt a dessiné le motif du sac à main. La chaise cornue est de Dialogica. Des dessins architecturaux de Piero Fornasetti ont été tendus sur le secrétaire Gio Ponti. Dans l'étagère de verre, des boules de verre et de marbre.

Above and facing page: in the combination bedroom and dressing room, fashion creations by Tom and Linda Platt. The embroidery on the yellow pillows and the decorative gathering of the velour bedspread was the labor of none other than Tom Platt himself. The picture of a handbag is by Linda Platt. The horned chair is by Dialogica. Architectural drawings by Piero Fornasetti are mounted on the Gio Ponti desk. Glass and marble spheres grace the glass shelves.

Oben und rechte Seite: Im Schlaf- und Ankleidezimmer findet sich Mode von Tom und Linda Platt. Die gelben Kissen hat Tom Platt selbst bestickt, den Bettüberwurf aus Velours höchstpersönlich gerafft. Das Handtaschengemälde ist ein Entwurf von Linda Platt. Der gehörnte Stuhl ist von Dialogica. Auf den Gio-Ponti-Sekretär sind Architekturzeichnungen von Piero Fornasetti aufgezogen. In dem Glasregal liegen Kugeln aus Glas und Marmor.

*Deux enfants, deux chiens, plusieurs chats n'empêchaient pas l'actrice
Isabella Rossellini de rêver sans cesse à un appartement où les matériaux nobles côtoieraient de délicates antiquités. Et puis elle a rencontré John Ryman qui partage maintenant sa vie. Designer, il est doté
d'un grand sens pratique et l'a aidée à remettre de l'ordre dans sa vie
et son appartement. Il arriva même un matin avec une camionnette
pleine de jolies choses, qu'ils placèrent et déplacèrent avant de les re-
charger dans la camionnette le soir, parce que rien ne convenait. Et
les jours des «encombrants», Isabella Rossellini allait faire un tour
dans les beaux quartiers avec ses enfants – cela paraît incroyable,
mais elle le raconte elle-même. Elle a fait ses meilleures trouvailles
près de la villa d'un célèbre designer de mode, un maniaque de la décoration, dont elle tait le nom, évidemment. Aujourd'hui, le loft assez
stérile autrefois est devenu un foyer confortable pour la petite famille,
sans oublier tous les animaux en bois et en peluche.*

Isabella Rossellini

Notwithstanding her two children, two dogs, and several cats, film-
star and model Isabella Rossellini always dreamed of having her
New York loft decorated with fine materials and quality antiques.
Then she met John Ryman, her present companion, a designer
with a practical sense who helped to reorganize her life and her
apartment. Once he actually drove up with a truck full of beautiful
pieces, which they moved all around the loft, only to reload them
that night, since they didn't fit. On special trash disposal days they
used to stroll with the children through wealthy suburbia, relates
Isabella. Her best finds were made near the country home of a well-
known fashion designer, naturally unnamed, who suffers from
redecoration mania. In the meantime, the slightly sterile loft has
become a comfortable home for the family and pets, both live and
artificial.

*Zwei Kinder, zwei Hunde, mehrere Katzen – dennoch träumte Film-
star und Model Isabella Rossellini immer davon, ihr New Yorker Loft
mit edlen Materialien und feinen Antiquitäten auszustatten. Bis sie
den Designer John Ryman traf, ihren jetzigen Lebensgefährten, der ihr
half, ihr Leben und ihre Wohnung neu zu ordnen. Das ging soweit,
daß er eines Morgens mit einem Kleinlaster voller schöner Dinge vor-
fuhr, die sie gemeinsam in der Wohnung hin- und herrückten, bis sie
abends alles wieder einluden, weil es doch noch nicht paßte. Und an
Sperrmülltagen schlenderten sie mit den Kindern durch die Vororte
der feinen Leute, wie Isabella Rossellini selbst erzählt. Am ergiebig-
sten war die Suche in der Nähe des Landhauses eines bekannten
Modedesigners, der sich immer wieder neuen Dekorationsorgien hin-
gibt und dessen Namen sie natürlich nicht preisgibt. Mittlerweile ist
der früher eher sterile Loft ein gemütliches Zuhause für die ganze
Familie – inklusive all der künstlichen Tiere aus Holz und Stoff.*

Page précédente: dans le salon d'habillage, au-dessus d'une commode ancienne en cerisier, une collection de chapeaux et de bibis à plumes des années 20 et 30.
Ci-dessus et à droite: Le salon est une véritable arche de Noé: trois petits singes (ne rien voir, ne rien entendre, ne rien dire) ornent les parements de fenêtre en bois. Dans l'étagère, toutes sortes d'animaux exotiques sculptés en bois et à côté, un éléphant de Bali. Une porte à glissières s'ouvre sur un coin-repos garni de coussins en toile suédoise; des éléphants dansent sur le papier peint.

Previous page: In the dressing room, above an antique cherry-wood dresser, a display of feather hats and hat ornaments from the 20s and 30s.
Above and right: The drawing room is a Noah's ark: three "see no evil, hear no evil, speak no evil" monkeys adorn the wooden cornices above the windows. On the shelves are wooden masks representing a variety of exotic beasts, adjacent an elephant from Bali. A sliding door opens into a cozy corner with Swedish sailcloth pillows and dancing elephants on the wallpaper.

Vorhergehende Seite: Im Ankleidezimmer ist über einer alten Kirschholzkommode eine Sammlung von Federhüten und Hutgestecken aus den 20er und 30er Jahren dekoriert.
Oben und rechts: Der Salon ist eine wahre Arche Noah. Drei Äffchen – nicht sehen, nicht hören, nicht sprechen – zieren die hölzernen Fenstervolants. Im Regal Holzmasken von allerlei exotischen Getier, daneben ein Elefant aus Bali. Eine Schiebetür erlaubt den Blick auf eine Kuschelecke aus schwedischen Segeltuchkissen, auf der Tapete tanzen Elefanten.

Le grand lit est surélevé – hors d'atteinte des petits chiens d'Isabella Rossellini. La grille en fer forgé, trouvaille de John Ryman, provient d'une église abandonnée du Connecticut.

The double bed is raised especially high to prevent Rossellini's little dogs from treating it as their own. John Ryman found the iron trellis in an abandoned church in Connecticut.

Das große Bett ist besonders hoch, damit Rossellinis kleine Hunde nicht hinaufspringen können. Das Gitterwerk aus Eisen hat John Ryman in Connecticut in einer verlassenen Kirche gefunden.

Ci-dessus: *L'étagère et la table de toilette sont en fer forgé; elles ont été dessinées par John Ryman. Pour réaliser les appliques murales et le lustre, il a en partie utilisé des objets trouvés dans une décharge «chic». Les os à ronger des chiens sont suspendus à l'étagère qui contient des produits de la maison Lancôme, pour laquelle Isabella Rossellini a longtemps travaillé.*
Page de droite: *dans la chambre à coucher, de vieilles photos de famille du clan italo-suédois Rossellini/Bergman. Sur la commode Empire américaine, un portrait d'Isabella Rossellini enfant.*

Above: *Bathroom shelves and sink are of iron and were designed by John Ryman as well. He built chandelier and candelabra using objets trouvés. Canine treats dangle from the shelves, which hold products by the cosmetic firm for which Rossellini worked for many years.*
Facing page: *In the bedroom a family tree with old family photos showing members of the Italian-Swedish Rossellini/Bergman clans. On the American Empire chest a portrait of Isabella Rossellini as a child.*

Oben: *Regal und Waschtisch im Bad sind aus Eisen, John Ryman hat sie entworfen. Für Leuchter und Wandlampen hat er teilweise Fundstücke von einer Edel-Müllkippe benutzt. Am Regal hängen Hundeknochen, im Regal sind Produkte der Kosmetikfirma angeordnet, für die Rossellini viele Jahre lang gearbeitet hat.*
Rechte Seite: *im Schlafzimmer ein Stammbaum aus alten Familienfotos des italo-schwedischen Rossellini-Bergman-Clans. Auf der amerikanischen Empire-Kommode ein Porträt von Isabella Rossellini als Kind.*

Artiste new-yorkais né en Grèce, Lucas Samaras a longtemps vécu dans une maison louée insignifiante, inconfortable et dépourvue d'ascenseur de la Upper West Side. Un jour, chargé de sacs en plastique, il commença à faire des allées et venues dans le Central Park. Il déménagea ainsi deux mois durant, jour après jour, sac après sac, jusqu'à ce que tous ses objets précieux, ses objets de verre, ses célèbres «boîtes», soient arrivés à bon port vingt pâtés de maisons plus loin, à Midtown dans un gratte-ciel luxueux. Le nouvel appartement gigantesque est situé au 62e étage: on n'entend pas le bruit de la rue et il faut des jumelles pour voir ce qui se passe en bas, les avions font de l'ombre quand ils survolent son atelier. Samaras vit et travaille pour ainsi dire au ciel, New York est à ses pieds. Le matin, le soleil vient le réveiller, un spectacle qu'il ne voudrait manquer pour rien au monde. Le soir, il peut regarder le soleil disparaître au-dessus de New Jersey. Samaras quitte rarement son univers, on le comprend.

Lucas Samaras

A native of Greece, the New York artist Lucas Samaras lived for many years in a nondescript tenement on the Upper West Side with no modern amenities. One day, he began to pack up plastic bags for a trek through Central Park. It took Samaras two long months to move, day after day, bag after bag, until he had toted all his precious creations, his glass objects and famous boxes twenty blocks away to a gigantic new apartment on the 62nd floor of a luxurious midtown skyscraper, where passing airplanes cast their shadows into his studio. It is so high that no street noise is heard and life below can only be observed with binoculars. In the morning, Samaras is awakened by the rising sun, a spectacle he never wants to miss, not even for one day. In the evening, he sees the sun melting away over New Jersey. No wonder Samaras seldom leaves his world in the sky.

Jahrelang lebte der in Griechenland geborene New Yorker Künstler Lucas Samaras in einem unscheinbaren Mietshaus in der Upper West Side, ohne Aufzug und Komfort. Eines Tages begann der Umzug in ein 20 Block entferntes Apartment in Midtown: Zwei Monate lang lief er mit Plastiktüten bepackt durch den Central Park, Tag für Tag und Tüte für Tüte schleppte er all seine Preziosen, seine Glasobjekte, seine berühmten Boxes in das riesige neue Apartment im 62. Stock eines luxuriösen Wolkenkratzers. Hier hat er Portier und Aufzug sowie Flugzeuge, die beim Vorbeifliegen einen Schatten in sein Studio werfen. Es liegt so hoch, daß man den Lärm der Straße nicht hört und das Leben dort unten nur mit dem Fernstecher beobachten kann. Samaras lebt und arbeitet quasi mit dem Himmel von New York zu seinen Füßen. Morgens weckt ihn die aufgehende Sonne, ein Schauspiel, das er keinen Tag verpassen möchte. Abends kann er die Sonne über New Jersey dahinschmelzen sehen. Kein Wunder, daß Samaras seine Welt hier oben nur selten verläßt.

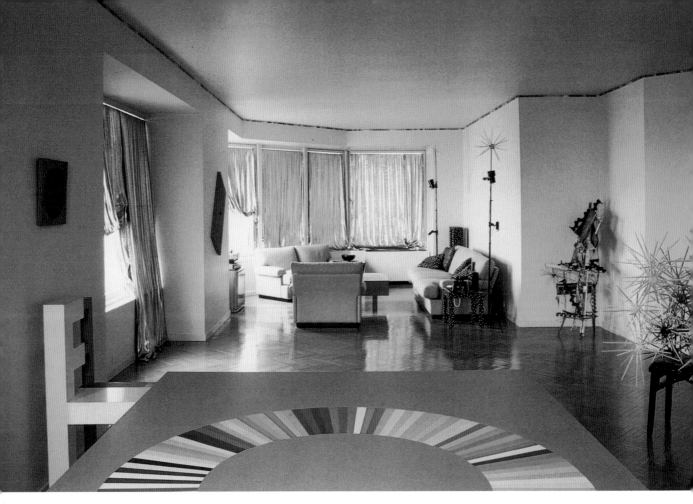

Page précédente: Au 62e étage, les rideaux argentés semblent encadrer le vide. Des colliers de perles de verre vénitiennes ornent le long corridor. En dessous, des œuvres de Samaras réalisées au cours des années 70.
Ci-dessus: vue sur le salon. Tables, lampes et sculptures sont de Samaras.
A droite: une des boîtes multicolores de Samaras, un collage ludique de fils, de bijoux fantaisie et de perles de verre.

Previous page: On the 62nd floor, metallic silver curtains seem to frame the sky. Chains of Venetian glass beads adorn the corridor walls. Below them are works by Samaras from the 70s.
Left: a view into the living room. Tables, lamps and sculptures are by Samaras.
Right: one of the colorful Samaras boxes, a playful collage of yarn, costume jewelry and glass beads.

Vorhergehende Seite: Die metallicsilbernen Vorhänge scheinen die Luft hoch oben im 62. Stock einzurahmen. Im langen Gang hängen Ketten aus venezianischen Glasperlen. Darunter Werke von Samaras aus den 70er Jahren.
Oben: Blick in das Wohnzimmer. Die Tische, Lampen und Skulpturen sind von Samaras.
Rechts: eine der bunten Samaras-Boxes, eine spielerische Collage aus Fäden, falschen Juwelen und Glasperlen.

Le paravent, le tableau, les chaises et la table du coin-repas sont de Samaras. Les coussins sont en plastique et bourrés de fils. Samaras s'assied rarement ici, il préfère une petite table de son atelier qui jouxte l'appartement. Des ceintures, des nœuds-papillons et des cravates sont suspendus dans l'ouverture du passe-plats.

Screen, picture, chairs and table in the dining area are by Samaras. The cushions are yarn-filled plastic. Only on rare occasions does Samaras sit here, prefering a small table in his studio, adjacent to his apartment. The convenience window into the kitchen displays belts, ties and bow ties.

Paravent, Gemälde, Stühle und Tisch im Eßbereich sind ebenfalls von Samaras. Die Plastikkissen sind mit Garn gefüllt. Nur selten sitzt der Künstler hier. Er zieht einen kleinen Tisch in seinem Studio vor, das sich an die Wohnung anschließt. In der Durchreiche zur Küche sind Gürtel, Fliegen und Krawatten angenagelt.

Tom Caccamo a dessiné les armoires vitrées qui surplombent le lit.
Elles abritent des objets en pierres précieuses et autres matériaux réalisés par Samaras au cours des années 60. Le tableau à gauche date
de 1985 et s'intitule «Le critique d'art».

The cabinets above the bed were designed by Tom Caccamo. They ac-
commodate objects from the 60s created by Samaras using gems and
other materials. The picture on the left is from 1985, and is entitled
"The Art Critic".

Die Vitrinen über dem Bett hat Tom Caccamo entworfen. Darin haben Samaras' Objekte aus Edelsteinen und anderen Materialien aus
den 60er Jahren ihren Platz gefunden. Das Bild links ist von 1985 und
heißt »Der Kunstkritiker«.

Au-dessus des assiettes sensationnelles de Samaras, une cohorte de
mariés en plastique, de ceux qui décorent les gâteaux de mariage.
D'autres étagères abritent des chaussures ornées de perles et de
pierres multicolores, ses petites et grandes boîtes, des verres et des
objets de verre – l'appartement est un musée réservé à cinq décennies
de son art.

Lined up on the shelf above the fanciful plates by Samaras is an army
of plastic wedding-cake figures. Other shelves display shoes decorated
with beads and colorful stones, Samaras' boxes of all sizes, glasses
and glass objects – the apartment is a museum of his art from five
decades.

Über den phantastischen Tellern von Samaras posiert eine Armee von
Hochzeitspaaren aus Plastik – Figuren, wie man sie auf Hochzeitstor-
ten findet. In anderen Regalen stehen mit Perlen und bunten Stein-
chen besetzte Schuhe, kleine und große Boxes, Gläser und Glasobjekte – das Apartment ist ein Museum für Samaras' Kunstwerke aus
fünf Jahrzehnten.

Jacqueline Schnabel, l'ex-épouse du peintre new-yorkais Julian Schnabel et mère de ses trois enfants, est née en Belgique, et vit depuis les
années 70 à New York. Quand on entre dans sa maison, on sent
immédiatement que vit ici une personnalité bohème et qui le reven-
dique, une cosmopolite au goût exquis. Bien que séparés depuis longtemps, Jacqueline et Julian Schnabel ont restauré, transformé et
meublé ensemble – et avec l'aide de David Piscuskas et Jürgen Riehm
de l'équipe 1100 Architects – cette maison urbaine édifiée au milieu
du siècle dernier à Greenwich Village. Jacqueline Schnabel a le don de
faire côtoyer négligemment des arrangements parfaits. Les tableaux
de Julian Schnabel et d'autres contemporains s'adaptent parfaitement au mobilier d'époques différentes, de l'Empire aux années 60.
Schnabel a lui-même mis la main à la maison qui abrite sa famille,
il a bétonné le sol de la cuisine, fabriqué la table à manger et soudé le
lit de fer de Jacqueline.

Jacqueline Schnabel

Jacqueline Schnabel, born in Belgium, has lived in New York since
the 1970s. She is the former wife of Julian Schnabel, New York
painter of fame, and the mother of their three children. When you
enter her house, you immediately have the feeling that this is the
residence of a bohemian in the best sense of the word, a cosmopolitan woman with exquisite taste. Although long divored, Jacqueline
and Julian Schnabel combined forces to restore, convert, and
furnish the Greenwich Village townhouse dating from the mid-19th
century, a task in which they were aided by David Piscuskas and
Jürgen Riehm of 1100 Architects. The house attests to the couple's
genius for perfect but relaxed arrangements. Paintings by Julian
Schnabel and contemporaries work perfectly with furniture of diverse eras, from Empire to the 1960s. Schnabel himself pitched in
to finish his family's residence, pouring the concrete kitchen floor,
making the dining table, and welding Jacqueline's iron bedstead.

Wenn man das Haus von Jacqueline Schnabel, in Belgien geboren,
seit den 70er Jahren in New York, Ex-Frau des New Yorker Malers
Julian Schnabel und Mutter seiner drei Kinder, betritt, hat man sofort
das Gefühl, daß hier eine bekennende Bohemienne lebt, eine Kosmopolitin mit exquisitem Geschmack. Obwohl lange geschieden haben
Jacqueline und Julian Schnabel das Mitte des vergangenen Jahrhunderts erbaute Stadthaus in Greenwich Village gemeinsam – und mit
Hilfe von David Piscuskas und Jürgen Riehm von 1100 Architects –
restauriert, umgebaut und eingerichtet. Das Haus lebt von ihrer
genialen Begabung, mit perfekten Arrangements lässig umgehen zu
können. Die Bilder von Julian Schnabel und Zeitgenossen harmo-
nieren bestens mit Möbeln aus verschiedensten Epochen, vom
Empire bis 60er Jahre. Schnabel selbst legte fleißig Hand an in dem
Haus, das seine Familie beherbergt, goß den Betonboden in der
Küche, schreinerte den Eßtisch und schweißte Jacquelines Eisenbett.

Premières pages: Jacqueline Schnabel et ses trois enfants dans le jardin de leur maison de Greenwich Village, qui a été complétée par une
galerie vitrée. La pièce de travail haute et lumineuse est peu meublée.
Ci-dessus: la chambre à coucher de Jacqueline Schnabel. Le papier
peint des années 40 montre des joueurs de base-ball. La cheminée
d'allure française a été coulée en plâtre.

First pages: Jacqueline Schnabel and her three children in the garden
of their townhouse in Greenwich Village, which was supplemented by
a glass pavilion. The high, light-flooded workroom is sparingly but
beautifully furnished.
Above: Jacqueline Schnabel's bedroom features baseball-pattern
wallpaper from the 40s. The French-style fireplace is a contemporary
plaster casting.

Erste Seiten: Jacqueline Schnabel und ihre drei Kinder im Garten
ihres Stadthauses in Greenwich Village, das durch einen gläsernen
Anbau ergänzt wurde. Spärlich möbliert das hohe lichte Arbeitszimmer.
Oben: Im Schlafzimmer von Jacqueline Schnabel eine Tapete aus
den 40er Jahren, auf der Baseball gespielt wird. Der französisch an-
mutende Kamin wurde neu aus Gips gegossen.

Ci-dessus: Dans la bibliothèque règne le même mélange de styles que dans toute la maison. Sur la cheminée, d'anciens vases chinois devant un nu de Tamara de Lempicka; une collection de fauteuils des années 40 et 50, une peau de vachette de l'Ouest américain.
Page suivante, à gauche: la chambre à coucher de Stella, la fille de Schnabel. Les rideaux des fenêtres et de la tête de lit sont pourpres.
Pages suivantes, à droite, de haut en bas et de gauche à droite: la salle de bains de Jacqueline Schnabel. Dans la salle de séjour règne un vaste lit-bateau. Un jaune souriant est une des couleurs principales de la maison. La cage d'escalier s'élance jusqu'au 5e étage.

Above: the library, in a stylistic mix typical of the enire residence. The mantelpiece displays antique Chinese vases in front of a Tamara de Lempicka nude. The collection of armchairs dates to the 40s and 50s, while the cowskin is perennial Wild West.
Following pages, left: daughter Stella's bedroom, with purple curtains at the windows and the head of her bed.
Following pages, right, clockwise from top left: the mistress of the house's bathroom. The living room is dominated by an enormous daybed. A friendly yellow is one of the keynote colors of the house. The stairway winds its way upwards through five floors.

Oben: die Bibliothek im typischen Stilmix des gesamten Hauses. Auf dem Kaminsims alte chinesische Vasen vor einem Akt von Tamara de Lempicka, Sesselsammlung aus den 40er und 50er Jahren, ein Kuhfell aus dem Wilden Westen Amerikas.
Folgende Seiten, links: das Schlafzimmer von Tochter Stella. Purpurfarben die Vorhänge vor den Fenstern und am Kopf ihres Bettes.
Folgende Seiten, rechts, im Uhrzeigersinn von links oben: das Bad der Hausherrin. Im Wohnzimmer dominiert ein überdimensional großes Tag-Bett. Freundliches Gelb ist eine der Hauptfarben des Hauses. Das Treppenhaus windet sich über fünf Stockwerke.

Une perspective de la chambre à coucher de Stella, qui séduit par son
ambiance romantique.

A view of the daughter's bedroom, which has a wonderfully romantic
atmosphere.

Ein Blick in das Schlafzimmer der Tochter, das durch seine romantische Atmosphäre besticht.

Au 5e étage, de vastes balcons avec vue sur le jardin de curé. Les carreaux du sol sont, comme presque partout dans la maison, des originaux réutilisés.

Spacious balconies on the top floor give a view into the enchanted garden. The tiles, as almost everywhere in the house, are original, having been freed of layers of paint and grime and resealed.

Im fünften Stock große Balkone mit Blick auf den verwunschenen Garten. Die Fliesen sind, wie fast überall im Haus, Originale, die freigelegt und neu versiegelt wurden.

Ci-dessus: *La cuisine du rez-de-chaussée est moderne et fonctionnelle. La cheminée qui couvre un pan de mur est en béton, la paroi du bar de cuisine est le derrière d'une porte.*
Page de droite: *Dans la grande cuisine se marient l'aluminium, l'albâtre, le bois et le béton. Julian Schnabel a fabriqué la table.*

Above: *The ground-floor kitchen is modern and functional. The man-high fireplace is cast concrete, the back wall of the kitchen counter is the back of a door.*
Right page: *Aluminium, alabaster, wood and concrete are the materials used in the spacious kitchen. The dining room table was built by Julian Schnabel.*

Oben: *Die Küche im Erdgeschoß ist modern und funktionell. Der mannshohe Kamin wurde aus Beton gegossen, die Rückwand der Küchentheke ist die Rückseite einer Tür.*
Rechte Seite: *Aluminium, Alabaster, Holz und Beton sind die Materialien der großen Küche. Den Eßtisch hat Julian Schnabel gebaut.*

New York Interiors   Jonathan Sheffer

Comparée aux magnifiques demeures historiques de la English Terrace situées en face, celle de Jonathan Sheffer, dans la West 10th Street, est plutôt banale. L'intérieur de cette maison construite en 1839 n'en est que plus inspiré. De la chambre sous les toits au quatrième étage, on entend la musique du compositeur résonner jusque dans les plus petits recoins. Une équipe d'architectes amis et de stylistes (Peter Pennoyer, Thomas Nugent, Michael Cox et Marianne Larsen) ont restauré avec précaution la maison où Sheffer reçoit régulièrement ses invités. Paul Bowles, l'écrivain et compositeur vivant à Tanger, y a séjourné – en 1995 Sheffer a pu le persuader de se rendre à New York pour la première fois depuis trente ans – pour assister au concert de ses œuvres que l'ensemble Eos de Sheffer a donné en son honneur au Lincoln Center. Leonard Bernstein a été l'un des maîtres de Sheffer qui est considéré comme l'un des jeunes compositeurs américains les plus innovants.

Jonathan Sheffer

Compared to the splendor of the historic English Terrace across the street, Jonathan Sheffer's brownstone house on West 10th Street seems rather plain. But the interior of his 1839 home is captivating. Resounding from the studio on the fourth floor under the roof, the composer's music fills every corner in the house, where up to a few years ago, a dentist had his practice. A team of Sheffer's friends, architects and designers Peter Pennoyer, Thomas Nugent, Michael Cox and Marianne Larsen, carefully renovated the structure, where Sheffer regularly entertains. One of his most notable house guests was the author and composer Paul Bowles from Tangier. Sheffer convinced him in 1995 to visit New York again, for the first time in thirty years, to attend a concert performed in his honor at the Lincoln Center by Sheffer's Eos Ensemble. Sheffer studied with Leonard Bernstein and others and is known as one of the most innovative young American composers.

Verglichen mit der Pracht der English Terrace, der historischen Häuser-reihe gegenüber, ist Jonathan Sheffers Brownstone an der West 10th Street eher nichtssagend. Um so stimmungsvoller ist das Innenleben des 1839 erbauten Hauses. Aus dem Dachstudio im vierten Stock schwingt die Musik des Komponisten bis in den kleinsten Winkel hinein. Fürwahr neue Töne, denn bis vor wenigen Jahren praktizierte hier ein Zahnarzt. Ein Team von befreundeten Architekten und Designern – Peter Pennoyer, Thomas Nugent, Michael Cox und Marianne Larsen – hat das Haus, in das Sheffer regelmäßig einlädt, behutsam renoviert. Bemerkenswerter Hausgast war Schriftsteller und Komponist Paul Bowles aus Tanger, den Sheffer überzeugen konnte, 1995 nach 30 Jahren zum ersten Mal wieder nach New York zu kommen – und zwar zu einem Konzert, das Sheffers Eos-Ensemble ihm zu Ehren im Lincoln Center gab. Sheffer hat unter anderem bei Leonard Bernstein studiert und gilt als einer der innovativsten jungen amerikanischen Komponisten.

Pages précédentes: *Douze colonnes doriques encadrent le petit jardin de Greenwich Villag dessiné par Madison Cox; le grand platane est protégé. Une autre terrasse sépare le jardin et la maison. La croûte de peinture noire, qui recouvre les volutes en fer forgé de l'escalier qui monte au quatriè étage, a été conservée à dessein.*
Page de gauche: *C'est au quatrième étage de la maison construite en 1839 que Sheffer, compositeur et chef d'orchestre, travaille. Son Steinway trône sur le tapis d'Aubusson. Le canapé est signé Jeffrey Bilhuber. L'étagère abritant les disques compacts est de John Ryman.*
Ci-dessus: *Le tapis et le canapé du salon sont de Jeffrey Bilhuber, la table basse de Paul Frankl. Les portes coulissantes s'ouvrent sur la salle à manger. Table de Chris Lehrecke, chaises pliantes de Warren McArthur. La cheminée du premier étage est en marbre noir. Un accrochage de photographies de Cindy Sherman, Bruce Weber, Robert Mapplethorpe et de dessins de John Singer Sargent et d'autres artistes.*

Previous pages: *The small garden in Greenwich Village was laid out by Madison Cox. It is framed by twelve Doric columns; the old plane tree is protected as a natural resource. Between garden and house there is also a terrace. The encrusted black paint on the iron ornaments of the steps in the winding staircase running through four storeys, was intentionally preserved.*
Facing page: *On the fourth floor of the 1839 brownstone is the composer-conductor's music studio. Sheffer's Steinway B grand piano and a sofa by Jeffrey Bilhuber stand on an Aubusson rug. The CD shelves are by John Ryman.*

Above: *Carpet and sofa in the salon are by Jeffrey Bilhuber, the coffee table is by Paul Frankl. Sliding doors lead into the dining room. The table is by Chris Lehrecke, the folding chairs by Warren McArthur. Near the black marble fireplace, on the first floor, is an art gallery where photos by Cindy Sherman, Bruce Weber and Robert Mapplethorpe supplement drawings by John Singer Sargent and others.*

Vorhergehende Seiten: *Den kleinen von Madison Cox gestalteten Garten in Greenwich Village rahmen zwölf dorische Säulen. Die große Platane ist denkmalgeschützt. Zwischen Garten und Haus liegt eine weitere Terrasse. Die schwarze Farbkruste der eisernen Schnörkel in den Stufen der sich über vier Stockwerke hochwindenden Treppe wurde absichtlich nicht abgelöst.*
Linke Seite: *Im vierten Stock des 1839 erbauten Brownstone befindet sich das Musikstudio des Komponisten und Dirigenten. Auf dem Boden ein Aubussonteppich, in der Mitte des Raumes ein Steinway-B-Flügel und außerdem ein Sofa von Jeffrey Bilhuber. Das CD-Regal hat John Ryman entworfen.*
Oben: *Teppich und Sofa im Salon sind von Jeffrey Bilhuber, der Kaffeetisch ist von Paul Frankl. Schiebetüren führen ins Eßzimmer. Tisch von Chris Lehrecke, Klappstühle von Warren McArthur. Der Kamin ist aus schwarzem Marmor, daneben eine Galerie mit Werken von Cindy Sherman, Bruce Weber, Robert Mapplethorpe und Zeichnungen unter anderem von John Singer Sargent.*

Ci-dessus et à droite: La cuisine au sous-sol s'ouvre sur une terrasse où l'on peut prendre les repas. Son équipement est digne d'un professionnel. Les chaises en tube proviennent d'un café parisien et entourent une table shaker américaine.
Page de droite: Les lambris de la chambre à coucher sont en bouleau huilé. Ils se trouvaient initialement deux étages plus bas, dans le salon où le dentiste, l'ancien propriétaire, a vécu cinquante ans. Les tables de nuit de John Ryman sont habillées du cuir qui revêtait les planches de rangement des anciens placards.

Above and right: The kitchen in the basement contains professional appliances and opens onto a dining patio. The aluminum chairs come from a café in Paris, and the white tablecloth conceals an American Shaker table.
Facing page: The oiled birchwood wall paneling in the bedroom was moved up two floors from the living room of the dentist who had resided in the house for half a century before its renovation. The night tables by John Ryman are covered in leather from the shelves of the old built-in closets.

Oben und rechts: Die Küche im Souterrain führt auf eine Eßterrasse und ist professionell ausgestattet. Die Aluminiumstühle stammen aus einem Pariser Café und stehen um einen amerikanischen Shaker-Tisch.
Rechte Seite: Die Wandtäfelung im Schlafzimmer ist aus geölter Birke und befand sich vor der Renovierung zwei Etagen tiefer, im Salon des Zahnarztes, der ein halbes Jahrhundert in dem Haus gewohnt hatte. Die Nachttische von John Ryman sind mit dem Leder bezogen, mit dem die Einlegeböden in den alten Einbauschränken ausgeschlagen waren.

Donald Trump, le grand magnat new-yorkais de l'immobilier, a toujours autant de plaisir à regarder par l'une des fenêtres hautes de 6,50 m de son palais privé dans la Trump-Tower, sur la Fifth Avenue à Manhattan: «Vous voyez là le Plaza Hotel, il est à moi. L'immeuble brun rayé de blanc, Trump Plaza, c'est à moi. Derrière, Wollman Rink, c'est à moi. En construction, le Trump International, c'est à moi. Superbe, n'est-ce pas? Malheureusement, on ne peut pas voir mes trois immeubles derrière le General Motors Building, trois autres, dont le Trump Palace, non plus.» Il vit avec sa famille tout en haut de la Trump Tower édifiée en 1983. Le 67e étage est réservé aux réceptions, le 68e abrite la suite personnelle du maître de maison et le 69e est le domaine de la famille qui profite aussi d'un jardin suspendu. Trump ouvre volontiers les portes de son palais de conte de fées. Et ses salons de style Louis XIV aménagés dans l'un des bâtiments les plus modernes du monde démontrent au mieux la véracité du leitmotiv américain «Anything goes».

Donald Trump

Whenever Donald Trump, the New York real estate tycoon, gazes down from one of the 6.50 m windows of his private palace in his Trump Tower on Fifth Avenue high above Manhattan, it's with the pride of ownership: "Look, down there, the Plaza Hotel, it's mine. The brown highrise with the white stripes, Trump Plaza, it's mine. Over there, Wollman Rink, it's mine. The one under construction, Trump International, it's mine. Really, isn't this a great view? Unfortunately my three skyscrapers behind the General Motors Building are not visible from here, along with three others, including Trump Palace." The Trump family resides on the top floors of the Trump Tower, built in 1983. The apartment is divided into an opulent entertaining area on the 67th floor, the 68th floor master suite of the owner, and the 69th floor, the family area, with a roof park. Trump's lavish residence exemplifies the American slogan "anything goes", even a palace in Louis XIV style in one of the most modern buildings in the world.

Wenn der Immobilien-Tycoon Donald Trump aus einem der 6,50 m hohen Fenster seines Privat-Palazzos in seinem Trump Tower an der Fifth Avenue hoch über Manhattan nach unten zeigt, ist ihm das immer wieder ein Riesenvergnügen: »Sehen Sie, da unten das Plaza Hotel: meines. Das braune Hochhaus, das mit den weißen Streifen, Trump Plaza: meines. Da hinten Wollman Rink: meines. Dort im Bau ist Trump International: meines. Sieht toll aus, nicht wahr? Meine drei Hochhäuser hinter dem General Motors Building kann man leider nicht sehen, drei weitere, unter anderem meinen Trump Palace, auch nicht.« Mit seiner Familie okkupiert er die obersten Stockwerke des Trump Tower, den er 1983 erbauen ließ. Das Apartment ist aufgeteilt in eine Repräsentationsetage im 67. Stock, die Mastersuite des Hausherrn im 68. und den Familienbereich mit Dachpark im 69. Stock. Trump zeigt seinen opulenten Märchenpalast gern: Er ist Beispiel für das amerikanische Leitmotiv »Anything goes« (Alles ist machbar) – sogar ein Palazzo im Louis-XIV-Stil in einem der modernsten Gebäude der Welt.

Premières pages: Du 67e étage, le regard effleure une console dorée garnie de photos de famille avant de glisser sur Central Park. Sur la photo de gauche on voit Donald et Marla Trump avec leur fille Tiffany.
Double pages précédentes: *Dans le salon Louis XIV, tout ce qui brille comme de l'or est de l'or, le bronze est du bronze. Les colonnes et les lambris sont en onyx. Au plafond, les fresques montrent des motifs célestes. Avant d'emménager en 1985, Donald Trump avait fait fabriquer tout à neuf. Un perfectionniste tel que lui n'a pu s'accommoder d'antiquités authentiques.*
Ci-dessus: *La lourde table marquetée en onyx de la salle à manger a dû être hissée avec une grue au 67e étage. Les oscillations, visibles et audibles, du lustre suivent les mouvements naturels du gratte-ciel.*
Page de droite: *La rampe ouvragée de l'escalier qui mène aux appartements privés est en bronze massif. Les tapis ont 4 cm d'épaisseur. Des paysages de ruines semblent se multiplier dans les vastes miroirs.*

First pages: *a view of Central Park from the 67th floor and a gold cabinet with family photos. Left: Donald and Marla Trump with their little daughter, Tiffany.*
Previous double pages: *In the opulent grand salon in Louis XIV style, gold is gold, bronze is bronze. Columns and wall paneling are onyx. The ceiling frescoes contain celestial motifs. When Trump moved into*

his apartment in 1985, everything was newly built. Genuine antiques were not perfect enough for the perfectionist.*
Above: *The heavy, inlaid onyx table in the baronial dining room had to be hauled to the 67th floor by crane. The chandelier continually oscillates with the natural movement of the skyscraper.*
Facing page: *Solid bronze bannisters adorn the staircase leading up to the private area. The carpets are more than 4 cm thick. Antique landscapes, depicting ruins, are multiplied in the large mirrors.*

Erste Seiten: *Aus dem 67. Stock schweift der Blick von einer goldenen Konsole mit Familienfotos hinaus über den Central Park. Links Donald und Marla Trump mit Töchterchen Tiffany.*
Vorhergehende Doppelseiten: *In der opulenten Wohnhalle im Louis-XIV-Stil ist Gold Gold. Säulen und Wandtäfelungen sind aus Onyx. Deckenfresken zeigen Himmelsmotive. Alles 1985 neu angefertigt, echte Antiquitäten waren dem Perfektionisten nicht perfekt genug.*
Oben: *Der Intarsientisch aus Onyx im Speisesaal mußte mit einem Kran in den 67. Stock gehievt werden. Der Kronleuchter bewegt sich sichtbar mit den natürlichen Schwingungen des Wolkenkratzers.*
Rechte Seite: *Das Geländer der Treppe, die in den privaten Bereich führt, ist aus massiver Bronze gefertigt. Die Teppiche sind 4 cm dick. Ruinenlandschaften vervielfachen sich in den großen Spiegeln.*

La chambre à coucher du maître de maison. Le lit Kingsize est coiffé
d'une couronne dorée, au centre de laquelle plane l'initiale T, joli-
ment arquée. Des anges gardiens veillent sur son sommeil. Sur la
table de nuit, « The 7 spiritual Laws of Success» (Les sept lois spiri-
tuelles du succès) de l'Indien Deepak Chopra, lecture de chevet de son
épouse, nous assure Trump, pragmatique bon teint.

The master's bedroom suite. The king-size bed has a gold headboard
with a calligraphed initial T – for Trump. Guardian angels watch over
his sleep. The book on the nighttable, "The Seven Spiritual Laws
of Success", was written by Deepak Chopra of India. Pragmatic Mr
Trump assures us that this is his wife's bedtime reading.

Die Schlafsuite des Hausherrn. Das King-size-Bett wird von einem
goldenen Kopfteil gekrönt, in dessen Mitte das hübsch geschwungene
Initial T – für Trump – schwebt. Schutzengel behüten seinen Schlaf.
Auf dem Nachttisch »The 7 spiritual Laws of Success« (Die 7 spiri-
tuellen Gesetze des Erfolgs) des Inders Deepak Chopra – die Nacht-
lektüre seiner Frau, wie der pragmatische Trump beteuert.

Ci-dessus: La bande vidéo pour garder la forme conçue par Marla est un best-seller; elle la passe dans son propre studio de gymnastique qui est en même temps la salle de jeux de Tiffany. La mère et la fille passent ici ensemble leurs matinées.
A droite: la salle de bains du maître de maison.

Above: Marla's fitness video, a bestseller, fills the screen in her own fitness studio, which does double duty as Tiffany's playroom. This is where mother and daughter spend their mornings together.
Facing page: the master's bathroom.

Oben: Marlas Bestseller-Fitness-Video läuft in ihrem eigenen Fitness-Studio, das gleichzeitig Spielzimmer von Tiffany ist. Dort verbringen Mutter und Tochter morgens gemeinsam ihre Zeit.
Rechts: das Badezimmer der Hausherrin.

Mary Ann Tsao, pédiatre née à Hong Kong, avait cherché des années durant une maison dans laquelle elle pourrait vivre et exercer son métier. Quand elle a eu enfin trouvé la maison qui lui convenait, une construction de trois étages datant de 1841, située à Greenwich Village et «restaurée» de manière indéfinissable, elle n'a plus eu qu'à la laisser aux bons soins de son frère. Pour l'architecte Calvin Tsao et son partenaire Zack McKown, cela devint un projet exaltant. Il s'agissait de marier la philosophie bouddhiste avec la passion du Dr. Tsao pour le surréalisme, les antiquités françaises, la Renaissance italienne, sans oublier les besoins des jeunes patients. Les idées de cette cosmopolite moderne ont été interprétées avec beaucoup de sensibilité: un salon néoclassique, une chambre à coucher néo-Renaissance, un temple bouddhiste pour la méditation, un bain japonais, une bibliothèque moderne et un escalier en colimaçon aux lignes hardies en acier doré ont vu le jour. Au rez-de-chaussée, un cabinet de pédiatre à l'ambiance joyeuse et la cuisine qui s'ouvre sur un jardin romantique.

Mary Ann Tsao

Dr Mary Ann Tsao, pediatrician and native of Hong Kong, searched for years for a building that would double as office and home. When she finally found the three-storey 1841 townhouse in Greenwich Village, she simply turned the clumsily renovated establishment over to her brother. Architect Calvin Tsao and his partner Zack McKown faced the challenge of bringing Buddhist philosophy, Dr Tsao's enthusiasm for Surrealism, French antiques, Italian Renaissance, and the needs of her little patients, all under one roof. The result was a sensitive blend: a neoclassical salon, Renaissance-style bedroom, Buddhist meditation temple, Japanese bathroom, modern library, and a bold winding staircase of gilded steel. On the ground floor, a cheerful pediatric practice and the kitchen leading to a romantic garden.

Die in Hongkong geborene Kinderärztin Dr. Mary Ann Tsao hatte jahrelang nach einem Haus gesucht, in dem sie praktizieren und leben konnte. Als sie endlich das 1841 erbaute, dreistöckige Stadthaus in Greenwich Village fand, konnte sie das verunstaltete Gebäude einfach ihrem Bruder überlassen. Für den Architekten Calvin Tsao und Partner Zack McKown wurde es ein spannendes Projekt. Buddhistische Philosophie sollte mit Tsaos Begeisterung für Surrealismus, französische Antiquitäten, italienische Renaissance und Bedürfnissen ihrer kleinen Patienten unter einen Hut gebracht werden. Entstanden ist eine sensible Interpretation der modernen Kosmopolitin: ein neoklassizistischer Salon, ein Neo-Renaissance-Schlafzimmer, ein buddhistischer Meditationstempel, ein japanisches Bad, eine moderne Bibliothek und eine kühne Wendeltreppe aus vergoldetem Stahl. Im Parterre eine fröhliche Kinderpraxis und die Küche, die in einen romantischen Garten führt.

Page précédente: L'escalier en colimaçon prend son essor au-dessus de la cheminée comme une sculpture moderne d'air et d'acier doré mat. Clin d'œil à Magritte: les portières en velours rouge, drapées en longs plis réguliers, semblent figées.

Page de gauche: pour amateurs de vertige. Les fines armatures de l'escalier tournant se poursuivent dans le sol de la bibliothèque et découvrent au regard l'habitat situé au-dessous.

Ci-dessus à gauche et à droite: Les chaises, 18e français, sont revêtues de crêpe de Chine. Une lampe-soleil darde ses rayons. Le sol est recouvert de carreaux de couleur, disposés en étoile. Méridienne en cerisier de Tsao/McKown.

Previous page: Above the fireplace, the lofty winding staircase resembles a modern sculpture of matte gold-plated steel and air. The precisely folded drapes of uncut red velvet look rigid and immobile and are reminiscent of René Magritte.

Facing page: vertigo? The fine grating of the winding stairs is continued in the library floor, permitting an unobstructed view of the living area below.

Above, left and right: The chairs, 18th-century France, are covered with Chinese silk. The solar-rag design of the ceiling lamp is complemented by the multicolored terrazzo floor in a star design. Cherrywood daybed by Tsao/McKown.

Vorhergehende Seite: Über dem Kamin schwebt die leichte Wendeltreppe wie eine moderne Skulptur aus mattgoldenem Stahl und Luft. Referenz an René Magritte: in akkurate Falten gelegt wirken die Portieren aus rotem Pannesamt wie erstarrt.

Linke Seite: schwindelfrei: die feinen Roste der Wendeltreppe setzen sich im Boden der Bibliothek fort und geben den Blick frei auf den darunterliegenden Wohnbereich.

Oben links und rechts: Die französischen Stühle aus dem 18. Jahrhundert sind mit chinesischer Seide bezogen. Von der Decke strahlt eine sonnige Lampe. Der Boden ist mehrfarbiger Terrazzo, sternförmig verlegt. Die Récamiere ist von Tsao und McKown in Kirschholz entworfen.

Ci-dessus : une pièce dans la pièce : le lit somptueux de Mary Ann Tsao, interprétation moderne de la Renaissance. Cadre et piédestal en cerisier, les voilages bien tendus de mousseline blanche lui rappellent les moustiquaires de son enfance à Hong Kong.
Page de droite : où la cheminée se fait œuvre d'art. Le cadre en acier doré est intégré dans un mur crépi à l'ancienne mode vénitienne par Anne Philippe.

Above: space within space: Mary Ann Tsao's magnificent bed is a modern Renaissance interpretation. Frame and platform are cherry wood, the taut white, very fine gauze veils remind the New York physician, who was born in Hong Kong, of the mosquito nets of her childhood.
Facing page: fireplace art: the gold-plated steel frame is embedded in the wall. The stucco was applied by Anne Philippe, using an old Venetian method.

Oben: Raum im Raum: Das prachtvolle Bett von Mary Ann Tsao ist eine moderne Renaissance-Interpretation. Rahmen und Podest sind aus Kirschholz, die weißen, straff gespannten Schleier aus feinster Gaze erinnern die in Hongkong geborene New Yorkerin an die Moskitonetze ihrer Kindheit.
Rechte Seite: Kamin als Kunst: Der Rahmen aus vergoldetem Stahl ist eingebettet in eine von Anne Philippe in alter venezianischer Manier verputzte Wand.

Outside of New York

Prosperous New Yorkers work in Manhattan from Monday to Friday, and as soon as the job allows, they leave the hustle and pollution of the city behind to spend the weekend in the country with the family. Every Friday at noon, lines of cars and limousines jam the streets on their way to tunnels and bridges crossing the Hudson and the East River. Trains and buses going to the country are packed. Helicopters take to the air off the 34th Street terminal, heading east and north to Upstate New York, New Jersey, along the Hudson, and to points in Connecticut, such as Greenwich. To the east and south are Fire Island, Long Island, East Hampton, Southampton, and all the small exclusive summer resorts on the Atlantic. New Yorkers with the required means have a second residence in the country. Within a radius of two or three hours by car, New Yorkers have restored the most beautiful farmhouses, remodeled abandoned schools, modernized magnificent old mansions, or realized their dreams of a house in the country in the latest architectural styles. As early as the late 80s the weekend out of town began to turn into a regular escape from the city. For many families, the house in the country has long since become a primary residence. Late Sunday evening or at the crack of dawn on Monday, the family provider returns to the city where, until next Friday, he lives alone in his city domicile, seeing the wife and kids only on the occasional visit.

Wer es in New York einigermaßen zu etwas gebracht hat, der arbeitet von Montag bis Freitag auf Manhattan und entflieht, so früh es der Job erlaubt, der Hektik und Verschmutzung der City, um mit Kind und Kegel das Wochenende auf dem Land zu verbringen. Und so sammelt sich jeden Freitagnachmittag überall in der Stadt eine Karawane von Limousinen, wälzt sich über die Brücken auf die andere Seite von Hudson und East River. Züge und Überlandbusse sind voll besetzt. Helikopter entschweben vom Terminal an der East 34th Street. Ost- und nordwärts streben sie nach Upstate New York, New Jersey, Greenwich, entlang des Hudson Rivers, hinauf nach Connecticut. West- und südwärts nach Fire-Island, nach Long Island, nach East- und Southampton und zu den anderen kleinen exklusiven Badeorten am Atlantik. Ein New Yorker, der es sich leisten kann, hat einen Zweitwohnsitz auf dem Land. Im Umkreis von bis zu drei Stunden Fahrt landauf, landab haben sie die schönsten Farmhäuser restauriert, verlassene Schulen umgebaut, prachtvolle alte Villen modernisiert oder sich in modernster Architektur ihren Traum vom Haus auf dem Land verwirklicht. Schon in den späten 80er Jahren begann sich der Wochenend-Trend zu einer regelrechten Stadtflucht weiterzuentwickeln. Für viele Familien ist das Haus auf dem Land längst zum ersten Wohnsitz geworden. Am späten Sonntagabend oder in aller Herrgottsfrühe am Montag macht sich der Familienernährer wieder auf zurück in die City, um bis zum nächsten Freitag allein das Stadt-Domizil zu bewohnen, das Kind und Kegel oft nur noch als Gäste sieht.

Celui qui a tant soi peu réussi à New York, travaille du lundi au vendredi à Manhattan et fuit ensuite, aussi vite que son travail le lui permet, les trépidations et l'air pollué de la ville, pour passer son week-end en famille à la campagne. C'est ainsi que l'on peut voir chaque vendredi dans toute la ville une caravane d'automobiles traverser les ponts et se déverser sur l'autre rive de l'Hudson et de la East River. Les trains et les cars sont bondés. Les hélicoptères s'élèvent au-dessus du terminal de la East 34th Street. A l'est et au nord, tous se dirigent vers Upstate New York, New Jersey, Greenwich, le long de l'Hudson, montent vers le Connecticut. Vers l'ouest et le sud, ils vont à Fire-Island, Long Island, à Easthampton et Southampton et les autres petites plages chic de l'Atlantique. Un New-Yorkais prospère possède une résidence secondaire à la campagne. Dans un rayon de jusqu'à trois heures de route à travers le pays ils ont ainsi restauré les plus belles fermes, adapté à leurs besoins les écoles abandonnées, modernisé les magnifiques vieilles villas ou bien ils ont réalisé dans l'architecture la plus moderne leur rêve de maison à la campagne. Dès la fin des années 80, la tendance à partir en week-end a évolué dans le sens d'un véritable exode urbain. La maison à la campagne est devenue depuis longtemps le domicile principal de nombreuses familles. Le dimanche soir, ou très tôt le lundi matin, le père de famille retourne en ville, et reste seul jusqu'au vendredi suivant dans son appartement où souvent le reste de la famille ne fait plus que de courts séjours.

Quand David Abelow, un élève du célèbre architecte new-yorkais
I.M. Pei, a été chargé de construire un atelier à Jersey pour un producteur de musique, ses qualités d'ingénieur de la construction lui ont
été aussi nécessaires que ses qualités d'architecte. Les salles de ce loft
gigantesque dans un hangar de Wells Fargo édifié en 1880 ont une
hauteur imposante de 15 m. Le grand espace ne comblait pas les
désirs du propriétaire qui voulait aussi une ambiance confortable. C'est
ainsi qu'Abelow, tout en soulignant vraiment le caractère industriel
des lieux, n'a pas hésité à le rompre en utilisant différentes essences
de bois aux tons chauds avec lesquels il a complété habilement les
poutres d'origine, vieilles de deux siècles. La chambre à coucher et la
salle de bain au premier étage, le studio d'enregistrement au second
sont placés sur des colonnes d'acier et sont reliés par un escalier.
L'espace habitable est demeuré aussi vaste qu'une salle des sports. Et
de fait, le producteur musical se détend parfois en jouant au basket.

David Abelow

David Abelow studied with the distinguished New York architect
I.M. Pei. When he was commissioned to build a studio for a music
producer in Jersey City, he needed the skills not only of an architect,
but also of a construction engineer. The ceilings of the gigantic
loft in an 1880 Wells Fargo warehouse reach the imposing height
of almost 15 m. Yet since comfort was a must, Abelow used
aluminum, steel and terrazzo to underline the industrial character
of the space, while lending it warmth with various woods that
complement the 200-year-old wooden beams. The result is a three-
storey house integrated in the loft, with bedrooms and bathroom
on the first floor, sound studio on the second floor. Supported by
steel columns, the two are connected by a grandiose curving staircase ramp. The living room is the size of a gymnasium, where in
fact the music producer sometimes unwinds by playing basketball.

Als David Abelow, Schüler des New Yorker Stararchitekten I.M. Pei,
den Auftrag erhielt, für einen Musik-Produzenten in Jersey City ein
Studio zu bauen, war er nicht nur als Architekt, sondern auch als
Bauingenieur gefordert. Der riesige Loft in einem 1880 erbauten
Lagerhaus von Wells Fargo verfügt über die imposante Raumhöhe
von 15 m. Bei aller Großzügigkeit wünschte der Eigentümer auch eine
wohnliche Atmosphäre. So unterstrich Abelow den Industrie-Charak-
ter einerseits mit Aluminium, Stahl und Terrazzo, andererseits brach
er ihn mit verschiedenen Hölzern in warmen Tönen, mit denen er
geschickt die 200 Jahre alten Originalbalken ergänzte. Entstanden ist
ein imposantes dreistöckiges Haus. Schlaf- und Badezimmer im
ersten, Tonstudio im zweiten Stock werden von Stahlsäulen getragen
und sind durch eine großzügig geschwungene Treppenrampe miteinander verbunden. Der Wohnraum ist so groß wie eine Sporthalle
geblieben. Und tatsächlich entspannt sich der Musik-Produzent
manchmal bei einem Basketballspiel.

Ci-dessus: Les différentes pièces du studio d'enregistrement sont regroupées au deuxième étage.
A droite: une variété remarquable de matériaux. Les escaliers en acier et les murs en planches de bois et en aluminium brossé, le plancher en bouleau finnois et les poutres bicentenaires constituent une maison dans la maison.
Double page suivante: L'espace habitable d'une hauteur de 15 m avec cuisine ouverte, est partagé en deux niveaux; la cage d'escalier de bois aux lignes élancées mène aux chambres à coucher.

Above: Various sound studio rooms are on the second floor.
Right: A remarkable variety of materials, such as steel staircases, walls built of wooden slats and brushed aluminum, floors made of Finnish birch and 200-year-old wooden beams form a house within a house.
Following pages: Within the large, almost 15 m high living area with an open kitchen, two floors were built. The curved wooden staircase leads to the sleeping area.

Oben: Im zweiten Stock sind die verschiedenen Räume des Tonstudios untergebracht.
Rechts: eine bemerkenswerte Vielfalt von Materialien. Treppen aus Stahl, Wände aus Holzlatten und gebürstetem Aluminium, Böden aus finnischer Birke und 200 Jahre alte Holzbalken bilden ein Haus im Haus.
Folgende Doppelseite: In den großen 15 m hohen Wohnraum mit offener Küche sind zwei Etagen eingezogen, das geschwungene Holztreppenhaus führt in den Schlafbereich.

Arlene Dahl fait partie de la légende hollywoodienne: elle a dansé avec Fred Astaire et donné la réplique à Bob Hope, Rock Hudson et Telly Savalas. Marc Rosen est le designer qui a signé des emballages devenus classiques pour Elizabeth Arden, Chloé, Halston etc. Mariés depuis treize ans, ils partagent une prédilection pour le style 19e. Trois ans avant leur mariage, Marc Rosen a découvert juste à côté de la rivière Hudson une demeure enchantée, construite en 1859 dans le style américano-victorien italiénisant typique de l'époque: coup de foudre partagé. Avec un grand savoir-faire et sans l'aide d'un décorateur, ils la firent restaurer, restituant à cette maison son atmosphère romantique. L'été dernier, Arlene Dahl a demandé à son fils Lorenzo Lamas, lui aussi une star hollywoodienne, ce qui lui ferait plaisir comme cadeau de mariage; il a souhaité des noces sur les rives de l'Hudson. Ce mariage, un événement mondain a même fait passer au second plan la réception de Noël qu'Arlene Dahl organise tous les ans.

Arlene Dahl and Marc Rosen

Arlene Dahl, legend of stage and screen, danced with Fred Astaire and co-starred with Bob Hope, Rock Hudson, and Telly Savalas. Marc Rosen designed the classic packaging for such clients as Elizabeth Arden, Chloé, Lagerfeld, and Halston. In their thirteenth year of marriage, the couple love 19th-century styles. Three years before their wedding, Marc Rosen discovered, right on the Hudson River, an 1859 mansion in the typical Italianate American-Victorian style of the period. With much skill and without an interior designer the couple had their refuge restored to its old, romantic state. Last summer, when Arlene Dahl asked her son Lorenzo Lamas, a successful Hollywood star like herself, what he would enjoy for his wedding, he said he would like to be married on the Hudson. It turned out to be a social event, outshining even the yearly Christmas reception at the Dahls.

Arlene Dahl ist die Hollywood- und Theaterlegende, die mit Fred Astaire tanzte und mit Bob Hope, Rock Hudson, Telly Savalas spielte. Marc Rosen ist der junge Designer, der Verpackungsklassiker für Elizabeth Arden, Chloé, Lagerfeld und Halston entwarf. Im 13. Jahr verheiratet teilen sie ihre Vorliebe für den Stil des 19. Jahrhunderts. Drei Jahre vor der Hochzeit entdeckte Marc Rosen direkt am Hudson River ein verwunschenes Mansion, das 1859 im amerikanisch-viktorianischen Stil erbaut worden war. Für beide war es Liebe auf den ersten Blick. Mit Sachverstand und ohne Innenarchitekt ließen sie es restaurieren und gaben ihrem Refugium die frühere romantische Atmosphäre zurück. Als Arlene Dahl ihren Sohn Lorenzo Lamas – wie sie ein erfolgreicher Hollywood-Star (»Falcon Crest«) – im letzten Sommer fragte, wie sie ihm zu seiner Hochzeit eine Freude machen könne, wünschte er sich ein Fest am Hudson. Es wurde ein gesellschaftliches Ereignis, das sogar den alljährlichen Dahlschen Weihnachtsempfang in den Schatten stellte.

Page de gauche: Le bardage dissimule un mur en chamotte, qui isole aussi bien de la chaleur que du froid.
Ci-dessus: Devant et derrière la maison, des vérandas ouvertes prolongent la salle à manger et le salon. Selon l'heure et l'ensoleillement, elles offrent des endroits ombragés.
A droite: Un miroir de la hauteur des murs agrandit encore l'entrée.

Facing page: Underneath the shingles the concealed firebrick masonry protects the house from heat and cold.
Above: Open verandas have been added to dining and living rooms in front and back of the house. Whatever the position of the sun, they provide shade at any time of the day and are used accordingly.
Right: At the entrance, a wall-size mirror gives the illusion of an elaborate foyer.

Linke Seite: Unter den Holzschindeln verbirgt sich Schamott, das vor Hitze und Kälte gleichermaßen schützt.
Oben: An Eßzimmer und Salon an der Vorder- und Rückseite des Hauses schließen sich offene Veranden an. Je nach Sonnenstand sind sie zu allen Tageszeiten schattige Plätze und werden entsprechend benutzt.
Rechts: Im Eingang vermittelt eine raumhohe Spiegelwand die Illusion eines großzügigen Foyers.

Arlene Dahl et Marc Rosen aiment recevoir pour le dîner. La porcelaine précieuse, les verres de cristal anciens et l'argenterie victorienne
sont alors à l'honneur.

Arlene Dahl and Marc Rosen like to have guests for dinner. Then the
table is set with valuable porcelain, antique crystal, and Victorian
silver.

Arlene Dahl und Marc Rosen haben gerne Dinnergäste. Dann wird
mit wertvollem Porzellan, altem Kristall und viktorianischem Silber
gedeckt.

New York Interiors   Arlene Dahl and Marc Rosen

A droite et ci-dessous: Dans le salon, les tonalités de sa vaste collection de porcelaine «aux roses» chinoise et française font écho au rose pâle et au soupçon de champagne des bergères et fauteuils en chintz et du tapis chinois. Les fenêtres sont garnies de stores de dentelle qui jouent selon l'heure avec les rayons du soleil ou la lumière des lampes.

Right and below: Pale rosé and a breath of champagne color Arlene's large collection of rose-patterned Chinese and French porcelain. These colors return in the salon in the chintz of the sofas and armchairs and in the Aubusson carpet. All windows have lace roll-up shades and, depending on the time of day, sunlight falling in or light penetrating to the outside present a romantic visual effect.

Rechts und unten: Ein blaßes Rosé und ein Hauch von Champagner, die Töne ihrer umfangreichen Sammlung chinesischen und französischen Porzellans mit Rosenmuster, kehren im kleinen Salon und im großen Wohnraum im Chintz der Sofas und Sessel sowie in dem Aubussonteppich wieder. Alle Fenster sind mit Spitzenrouleaus versehen, was je nach Tageszeit ein romantisches Lichtspiel zwischen den hereinfallenden Sonnenstrahlen und der effektvollen künstlichen Beleuchtung bewirkt.

Ambiance ludique dans la chambre à coucher d'Arlene Dahl. Mère attentive, elle l'a abandonnée récemment à son fils, le comédien Lorenzo Lamas et sa jeune épouse, le mannequin Shaun Sand, pour leur nuit de noces.

Playful atmosphere in Arlene Dahl's bedroom. Recently, after a big wedding party, the solicitous mother surrendered the room to her son, Lorenzo Lamas, and his new bride, photomodel Shaun Sand, for their wedding night.

Verspielte Atmosphäre im Schlafzimmer von Arlene Dahl. Kürzlich überließ sie es – ganz fürsorgliche Mutter – ihrem Sohn Lorenzo Lamas und seiner Braut, Fotomodell Shaun Sand, für die Hochzeits-nacht.

New York Interiors   Arlene Dahl and Marc Rosen

La baignoire plus que centenaire a passé des décennies dans une grange. Ses pieds ont été dorés; on a installé une robinetterie dorée; le revêtement extérieur a pris des allures de marbre. A l'instar des femmes du monde du 19e qui recevaient dans leur salle de bains, Arlene Dahl a fait de la sienne un salon avec cheminée et fauteuils.

The bathtub, more than a hundred years old, had been stored away in a barn for decades. The feet were gilded, gold fixtures installed, the surface marbleized. Like the baths, where 19th-century grande dames held court, Arlene Dahl's bathroom with fireplace and a group of seats has the appearance of a salon.

Die über 100 Jahre alte Wanne war jahrzehntelang in einer Scheune abgestellt. Die Füße wurden vergoldet, eine Goldarmatur installiert, die Außenschicht marmorisiert. Mit Kamin und Sitzgruppe ausgestattet, gleicht Arlene Dahls Badezimmer eigentlich einem Salon. Das läßt an die Salondamen des 19. Jahrhunderts denken, die in ihrem Bad regelrecht hofhielten.

Elle est originaire de Hollande et a travaillé des années comme top-model, ce qui l'a fait beaucoup voyager. Aujourd'hui elle est une styliste de mode à qui le succès sourit. Lui vient d'Écosse, écrit des textes traitant d'architecture et de culture, et cherchait aussi un coin tranquille où se poser. Fatigués de la grande ville, ils avaient la nostalgie d'un coin de verdure, pas trop loin de New York, où ils pourraient vivre et travailler ensemble. Ils ont trouvé un endroit romantique près de la ville universitaire de Princeton: c'est une usine désaffectée de la Atlantic Terracotta Company située au milieu d'un petit bois et près d'un ancien canal aux eaux tranquilles. Les architectes new-yorkais Smith-Miller et Hawkinson ont procédé à des transformations subtiles. La plate-forme de bouleau reposant sur des poutres gigantesques a une fonction essentielle. Elle divise la grande salle d'usine en deux niveaux, sans que les belles dimensions de la salle et la lumière qui pénètre par les immenses parois vitrées n'en pâtissent.

Barbara de Vries and Alastair Gordon

Barbara de Vries comes from Holland and, as a top model, once spent most of her time traveling. Now she is a successful fashion designer. Alastair Gordon of Scotland writes about architecture and cultural themes. Weary of the big city, both longed for a place in the country, but not too far from New York, where they could live and work together. In the university town of Princeton, an old factory building of the Atlantic Terracotta Company became their romantic retreat, in the middle of a small forest, not far from the quiet flow of an old canal. The New York architects Smith-Miller and Hawkinson worked out the clever reconstruction. A central function was allocated to the birchwood platform, resting on formidable beams. It divides the large factory hall into two levels without diminishing the sense of spaciousness and light.

Sie stammt aus Holland und war als Topmodel jahrelang nur unterwegs. Jetzt arbeitet sie als erfolgreiche Modedesignerin. Er kommt aus Schottland, schreibt über Architektur und Kultur und suchte ebenfalls einen ruhigen Platz. Der Großstadt überdrüssig sehnten sie sich nach einem Platz im Grünen, nicht zu weit entfernt von New York, nicht zu ländlich, zum gemeinsamen Leben und Arbeiten. In dem alten Fabrikgebäude der Atlantic Terracotta Company in der nahen Universitätsstadt Princeton haben die beiden inmitten eines Wäldchens und unweit eines still dahinfließenden alten Kanals ein romantisches Fleckchen gefunden. Den raffinierten Umbau besorgten die New Yorker Architekten Smith-Miller und Hawkinson. Zentrale Funktion kommt der auf gewaltigen Balken ruhenden Plattform aus Birkenholz zu. Sie teilt die große Fabrikhalle in zwei Ebenen, ohne daß die Großzügigkeit des Raumes und das Licht, das durch die riesigen Fensterfronten fällt, verlorengehen.

Page de gauche: Construite en 1894, la fabrique de la Atlantic Terra-cotta Company est située dans un endroit tranquille près de Prince-ton, dans le New Jersey.
Ci-dessus: Une paroi coulissante transparente sépare l'espace privé couvrant deux étages du grand hall vide et non chauffé. Ici, Iain, le fils des propriétaires, peut s'ébattre à son aise, et en outre, on économise de l'énergie. Le soir naissent de fantastiques jeux de lumière. Le sol est recouvert de ciment fin, les plafonds de toile ignifugée.

Facing page: The 1894 factory building of the Atlantic Terracotta Company stands near a quiet canal on the outskirts of the university town of Princeton, New Jersey.
Above: A transparent sliding wall separates the two-storey living and bedroom area from the large unheated entrance hall. This is a play space for son Iain and also an energy saver. In the evening the panels project fantastic light effects. The floor is of fine poured cement, the ceilings are lined with fireproof canvas.

Linke Seite: Die 1894 erbaute Fabrik der Atlantic Terracotta Com-pany steht an einem stillen Kanal außerhalb der Universitätsstadt Princeton, New Jersey.
Oben: Eine transparente Schiebewand trennt den zweigeschossigen Wohn- und Schlafbereich von der leeren, unbeheizten Eingangshalle. Hier kann Sohn Iain sich austoben, außerdem wird Energie gespart. Abends ergeben sich phantastische Lichtspiele. Der Boden besteht aus feinem gegossenem Zement, die Decken sind mit feuerfester Lein-wand ausgeschlagen.

Ci-dessus: Dans la cuisine règnent l'aluminium, l'ardoise et le bois.
La table est un ancien établi anglais du 19e siècle. Un grand tapis de
sisal habille le sol de ciment du salon et de la salle à manger.
Page de droite: Un lit de cuir spacieux des années 20 sert de lieu de
repos. La charpente n'est pas dissimulée, la lumière peut ainsi entrer
sans entraves par les grandes fenêtres de l'atelier. L'escalier mène aux
zones de repos et de travail.

Above: The kitchen surfaces are aluminum, slate and wood. The
dining table is an English workbench from the 19th century. A large
sisal rug covers the cement floor in the living and dining areas.
Facing page: A wide leather bed from the 20s invites relaxation. In
the factory hall a free-standing beam construction permits an abund-
ance of light to enter through the large studio windows. The staircase
leads to the bedroom and work area.

Oben: Die Küche ist in den Materialien Aluminium, Schiefer und
Holz gehalten. Der Eßtisch ist eine alte englische Werkbank aus dem
19. Jahrhundert. Auf dem Zementboden im Wohn- und Eßbereich
liegt ein großer Sisalteppich.
Rechte Seite: Ein breites Lederbett aus den 20er Jahren dient als
Ruheplatz. Die Balkenkonstruktion ist frei in die Fabrikhalle gestellt,
damit reichlich Licht durch die großen Atelierfenster einfallen kann.
Die Treppe führt in den Schlaf- und Arbeitsbereich.

Page de gauche et ci-dessus: travail sur les hauteurs. L'atelier de
Barbara de Vries, qui conçoit ici ses modèles; à côté, le bureau
d'Alastair Gordon, auteur et critique. Des panneaux coulissants en
bois de bouleau permettent de multiples agencements spatiaux.
A droite: La chambre à coucher est éclairée par la partie supérieure
de la fenêtre de l'atelier. La face arrière est tendue de toile, le plafond
souplement drapé. A l'arrière-plan, l'ancien mur de brique sombre.

Facing page and above: work, so to speak, on the platform. The
studio of Barbara de Vries, who designs her fashions here, adjoins the
office of Alastair Gordon, author and critic. The sliding birchwood
panels permit new room arrangements at any time.
Right: The bedroom receives light from the upper part of the studio
windows. Natural canvas sets the keynote of back wall and ceiling,
contrasting with the original dark brick wall.

Linke Seite und oben: Arbeiten sozusagen auf dem Podest: das
Atelier von Barbara de Vries, die hier ihre Mode entwirft. Nebenan
befindet sich das Büro von Alastair Gordon, dem Autor und Kritiker.
Verschiebbare Paneele aus Birkenholz ermöglichen immer wieder
neue Raumkonstellationen.
Rechts: Das Schlafzimmer erhält Licht durch den oberen Teil der
Atelierfenster. Die Rückwand ist mit Leinwand bespannt, die Decke
mit Leinwand abgehängt. Im Hintergrund kommt altes dunkles
Backsteingemäuer zum Vorschein.

Villa Amore, c'est ainsi que Richard et Elaine Ekstract ont baptisé leur maison de Sagaponack à Long Island. Pour Philip Johnson, cet ensemble de hall central, de campanile, de phare et de plate-forme observatoire, avec une piscine en forme de mandoline et un garage coiffé de gazon, est un «village parfait».

Richard and Eileen Ekstract call their home in Sagaponack, Long Island, "Villa Amore". "A perfect village", said architect Philip Johnson of the ensemble of central hall, campanile, lighthouse and observation platform, with a swimming pool shaped like a mandolin, and a garage with a grass roof.

»Villa Amore« nennen die Eigentümer Richard und Elaine Ekstract ihr Haus in Sagaponack auf Long Island. Als »ein perfektes Dorf« bezeichnete Philip Johnson das Ensemble aus Mittelhalle, Campanile, Leuchtturm und Aussichtsplattform, das über einen Swimmingpool in Form einer Mandoline und eine Garage mit Grasdach verfügt.

New York Interiors   Richard Ekstract

Richard Ekstract édite le magazine américain «Events»; Elaine, son épouse, est la propriétaire du «Mephisto», un magasin de chaussures chic à East Hampton. Un jour, ils ont eu envie d'autre chose et ont osé construire à Sagaponack, Long Island, berceau de nouveautés en matière d'architecture, une transposition ultramoderne du palais toscan. C'est ainsi qu'est née la «Villa Amore», un ensemble spectaculaire: dans un espace habitable de 2500 m² carrés, seule la chambre à coucher du maître des lieux paraît bien étriquée avec ses 18 m². C'est presque la seule critique qu'il profère à l'encontre des deux jeunes architectes, Diana Agresta et Mario Gandelsonas, qu'il a chargés de ce travail et propulsés ainsi au rang de stars. Le décorateur Paul Siskin n'a pas eu la tâche facile. Alors que les architectes pensaient que la maison, de par sa situation au milieu de la nature, n'avait pour ainsi dire pas besoin de mobilier, lui voulait la rendre aussi agréable à vivre. Les Ekstract qui changeaient autrefois de maison comme d'autres de chaussures, habitent déjà depuis cinq ans dans leur villa d'amour.

Richard Ekstract

Richard Ekstract is publisher of the US magazine "Events"; his wife Elaine has a posh shoestore in East Hampton. They both had their hearts set on something new. In Sagaponack on Long Island, where new architecture is thriving, they took the plunge and built an ultramodern version of a Tuscan palazzo, their "Villa Amore". Totalling 2500 sq.m., the only relatively small living space is the master bedroom, measuring only 18 sq.m. This disproportion was almost Ekstract's only criticism of the design, which made the New York architect-team Diana Agrest and Mario Gandelsonas into instant stars. Interior designer Paul Siskin, with an eye to the exquisite natural surroundings, has provided comfort without clutter. The Ekstracts used to change homes as others change their shoes. Now, they are in their fifth year in their villa of love, by the lake.

Richard Ekstract verlegt das amerikanische Magazin »Events«, seiner Frau Elaine gehört ein schickes Schuhgeschäft in East Hampton. Beide hatten Lust auf Neues, und so wagten sie in Sagaponack auf Long Island, einem Nährboden neuer Architektur, die ultramoderne Umsetzung eines toskanischen Palazzo. Es entstand ihre »Villa Amore«, ein spektakuläres Hausensemble. Bei 2500 m² Wohnfläche ist einzig das Schlafzimmer des Hausherrn mit 18 m² unverhältnismäßig klein. Dies ist beinahe seine einzige Kritik an der Arbeit des jungen New Yorker Architektenteams Diana Agrest und Mario Gandelsonas, die er mit seinem Auftrag zu Shooting-Stars machte. Interior-Designer Paul Siskin hatte keine leichte Aufgabe. Während die Architekten der Meinung waren, daß das Haus wegen seiner exquisiten Lage mitten in der Natur so gut wie keine Einrichtung bräuchte, wollte er es doch auch gemütlich machen. Der Kompromiß ist gelungen. Ekstracts, die vorher ihre Häuser wechselten wie andere ihr Schuhwerk, wohnen nun schon im fünften Jahr in ihrer Liebesvilla am See.

Ci-dessus et page de droite: vue sur la bibliothèque et le séjour. La porte à gauche, en acajou mat avec mosaïque de verre, lampes de Fran Taubman, une jeune designerin de Long Island. Le corps de l'imposant escalier en colimaçon largement déployé est en fer. Le tableau, en arrière-plan, est l'œuvre du peintre philippin Manuel Ocampo, les sculptures et la table sont un groupe du sculpteur espagnol Juan Munoz.

Above and facing page: view of library and living area. The door on the left is of matte mahogany with glass mosaic, the lamps are by Fran Taubman, a young Long Island designer. The splendid, sweeping spiral staircase is an iron-based construction. The picture in the background is a work by the Philippine painter Manuel Ocampo, the work on the stairway landing by the American painter Sheryl Laemle, sculptures and table are a group by the Spanish sculptor Juan Munoz.

Oben und rechte Seite: Blick in Bibliothek und Wohnhalle. Die Tür links ist aus mattiertem Mahagoni mit Glasmosaik, die Lampen stammen von Fran Taubman, einer auf Long Island ansässigen jungen Designerin. Der Körper der weit geschwungenen repräsentativen Wendeltreppe besteht aus Eisen. Das Gemälde im Hintergrund ist ein Werk des philippinischen Malers Manuel Ocampo. Die Skulpturen und der Tisch sind als Gruppe von dem spanischen Bildhauers Juan Munoz gearbeitet worden.

Page de gauche: La salle de séjour au plafond de bois voûté évoque une salle de gymnastique. Au milieu, un bloc-cheminée, fauteuils et canapé de Jean-Michel Frank, tables basses d'Alan Moss, tapis de Philippe Starck, table à pieds en spirales de fer de Fran Taubman, sculpture avec échiquier de Munoz, sculpture sur le manteau de cheminée de l'Anglais David Mach, profil près de la cheminée du Japonais Kenji Fujita.

Ci-dessus: le salon du soleil. Des ottomanes en tissu et cuir ainsi que les fauteuils dont le style s'inspire de l'Art Déco ont été dessinés par Paul Siskin qui a aménagé la maison. Près de la cheminée, un tableau de Jonathan Adolphe; en dessous, un banc de teck ancien originaire d'Indonésie.

Facing page: The living area with its vaulted wooden ceiling recalls a gymnasium. In the center a fireplace block, armchairs and sofa by Jean Michel Frank, side tables by Alan Moss, carpet by Philippe Starck, table with iron-spiral feet by Fran Taubman, sculpture with board by Munoz, sculpture on the mantel by David Mach of England, profile next to the fireplace by Kenji Fujita of Japan.

Above: the sun salon. The ottomans of fabric and leather and the armchairs, reminiscent of French Art Deco, were designed by Paul Siskin, the interior decorator for the home. The picture next to the fireplace is by Jonathan Adolphe, below it an antique teak bench from Indonesia.

Linke Seite: Die Wohnhalle mit der gewölbten Holzdecke erinnert an eine Turnhalle. In der Mitte ein Kaminblock, davor Sessel und Sofa von Jean Michel Frank sowie Beistelltische von Alan Moss. Auf dem Boden liegt ein Teppich von Philippe Starck. Der Tisch mit Füßen aus Eisenspiralen ist von Fran Taubman, darauf eine Skulptur mit Brett von Munoz. Die Skulptur auf dem Kaminabsatz stammt von David Mach aus England, das Profil neben dem Kamin von Kenji Fujita aus Japan.

Oben: Blick in den Sonnen-Salon. Ottomane aus Stoff und Leder sowie dem Stil des französischen Art déco nachempfundene Sessel sind ein Entwurf von Paul Siskin, der das Haus einrichtete. Das Gemälde neben dem Kamin ist von Jonathan Adolphe, darunter steht eine alte Teakholzbank aus Indonesien.

La salle à petit déjeuner: les chaises viennent du rayon meubles de Bloomingdale, New York. La table d'étain non polie repose sur une structure de bois ancienne (création de Taubman). On aperçoit sur la droite quelques-unes des dix-sept portes en verre à deux battants qui encadrent la maison.

The breakfast room. Chairs are from the New York department store Bloomingdale's. The brushed pewter table top is supported by a wooden substructure designed by Taubman. Visible on the right, some of a total of 17 double-winged glass doors that engender a merger of interior and exterior space.

Das Frühstückszimmer: Stühle aus der Möbelabteilung eines New Yorker Kaufhauses. Die geraute Tischplatte aus Zinn liegt auf einem alten Holzgestell nach einem Entwurf von Taubman. Rechts sind einige der insgesamt siebzehn zweiflügeligen Glastüren zu sehen, die das Haus zur Landschaft hin öffnen.

Le maître de maison trouve trop petite sa chambre à coucher de
18 m². Il a ramené de Goa le Jésus ancien sculpté. La sculpture au
néon au-dessus du lit est de Micah Lexier, le canapé en lèvres rouges
de Kristian Gavoille, un jeune designer français. Cette chambre de
maître se trouve dans le «phare», une porte de verre (invisible sur la
photo) mène par une passerelle de bois au Gazebo, un belvédère
pour les soirées intimes avec vue sur le lac Sagg.

The 18 sq.m. bedroom is too small for the master of the house.
Ekstract brought the antique Christ figure back from Goa. The neon
sculpture above the bed is by Micah Lexier. This room lies in the
"lighthouse" of the ensemble; a glass door, not in the photograph,
opens to the wooden bridge leading to the gazebo, where the Ekstracts
spend summer evenings overlooking Sagg Lake.

Das 18 m² große Schlafzimmer ist dem Hausherrn zu klein. Es liegt in
dem »Leuchtturm« des Ensembles, eine Glastür (nicht im Foto)
führt auf den hölzernen Steg zum Gazebo, der Aussichtsplattform für
lauschige Abende mit Blick über den Sagg-See. Die alte Jesusfigur
hat Ekstract aus Goa mitgebracht. Die Neonskulptur über dem Bett
ist von Micah Lexier.

C'est à Ephratah, un petit village de l'Upstate New York, que le sculpteur et designer new-yorkais Rico Espinet – il a entre autres équipé les
grands magasins Bergdorf Goodman et Henri Bendel de systèmes lumineux – et son épouse Heloisa Zero, dessinatrice, ont trouvé refuge.
Le bâtiment de brique rouge agrémenté de boiseries blanches et d'un
toit d'étain aux reflets d'argent pâle a été construit en 1929, et l'école
qu'il abritait fermée en 1979. Les pièces sont gigantesques, à la joie
des deux créateurs, qui se partagent un appartement pas très vaste à
Brooklyn. 1525 m² de surface d'habitation. Un couloir, long comme
une piste de bowling, divise la maison en son centre, à droite initialement les trois grandes salles de classe, à gauche deux toilettes et la
maternelle, au bout une petite cuisine et la grande salle des sports
jaune d'or au toit voûté. Quand le couple a acheté l'école en 1985,
les vandales étaient passés par là, détruisant les meubles, souillant
les murs. Pourtant, ils eurent tout de suite un coup de cœur.

Rico Espinet and Heloisa Zero

In the small town of Ephratah in upstate New York, the New York
sculptor and light designer Rico Epinet and his wife Heloisa Zero,
graphic designer, found their refuge. The white-trimmed red brick
schoolhouse with tin roof shimmering in pale silver, was built in
1929 and served its purpose until 1979. The creative partners, who
also have a modest apartment in Brooklyn, were attracted by the
imposing living space of 1525 sq.m. A corridor as long as a bowling
alley divides the building down the middle. On the right are three
former classrooms, on the left two washrooms and kindergarten,
at the end of the hallway a small kitchen and the spacious gymnasium, golden-yellow under a vaulted ceiling. Though abandoned and
vandalized, the school immediately fascinated the couple, who
bought it in 1985.

In dem kleinen Ort Ephratah, Upstate New York, haben der New
Yorker Bildhauer und Licht-Designer Rico Espinet und seine Frau, die
Grafikerin Heloisa Zero, ihr Refugium gefunden. Das alte Haus aus
rotem Backstein mit weißem Holzwerk und blaßsilbern schimmern-
dem Zinndach wurde 1929 erbaut und diente bis 1979 als Schule. Die
Raumdimensionen sind gewaltig – zur Freude der beiden Kreativen,
die ansonsten ein nicht sehr großes Apartment in Brooklyn bewohnen. Hier stehen ihnen 1525 m² Wohnfläche zur Verfügung. Ein Gang,
so lang wie eine Bowling-Bahn, teilt das Gebäude in der Mitte.
Rechts befinden sich die drei ehemaligen Klassenräume, links zwei
Waschräume und der frühere Kindergarten, am Ende des Ganges eine
kleine Küche und eine große goldgelbe Sporthalle mit gewölbter
Decke. Als die beiden 1985 die verlassene Schule erwarben, hatten
Vandalen ihr widerliches Spiel getrieben, die Möbel zerschlagen und
die Wände verschmiert. Es war dennoch Liebe auf den ersten Blick.

Ci-dessus: Comme autrefois, la porte de derrière de l'école du village construite en 1929 mène au gymnase, si vaste que l'on peut y faire des tours à bicyclette. Ici, le temps a bien travaillé: la patine des murs jaune d'or ne pourrait pas être plus chaude.
A droite: vue sur la forêt d'épicéas que les écoliers d'Ephratah ont plantée en 1941. Les propriétaires des lieux ont l'intention d'aménager plus tard un étang dans les parages.

Above: Unchanged, the back door of the 1929 village school opens to the gymnasium, big enough for a little bike riding. Time need not ravage: the golden-yellow patina on the walls could not be more warm and beautiful.
Right: view of a spruce forest, planted in 1941 by the school children of Ephratah. The house owners have future plans for digging a pond nearby.

Oben: Wie schon früher führt die hintere Tür der 1929 erbauten Dorf-schule in das »Gymnasium«, die Sporthalle, die groß genug ist für gelegentliche Extratouren auf dem Fahrrad. Die Zeit hat in diesem Fall gute Arbeit geleistet: Die Patina der goldgelben Wände könnte nicht wärmer sein.
Rechts: Blick auf einen Fichtenwald, den die Schulkinder von Ephratah im Jahr 1941 angepflanzt haben. In der Nähe wollen die Hausbesitzer später einmal einen Teich anlegen.

Page de gauche: Sur la table de la bibliothèque, dessins de Rico Espinet, objets trouvés et boîtes à cigarres forment une œuvre d'art totale.
Ci-dessus: Espinet a transformé directement deux des trois grandes salles de classe en ateliers. L'un est réservé aux gros travaux, l'autre (photo) aux finitions.
A droite: Les vandales s'en étaient donné à cœur joie, ne laissant rien de l'ameublement d'origine. Heloisa Zero a chiné dans les villages voisins des meubles tout simples, comme cette chaise. Lampadaire de Rico Espinet, dans le petit placard mural, la corde de la vieille cloche de l'école.

Facing page: on the library table, a work of art composed of designs by Rico Espinet, found objects and cigar-boxes.
Above: Two classrooms were converted into studios, one for rough work, the other (photo) for the finishing touches.
Right: Vandals had completely destroyed the original school furniture. So Heloisa Zero went bargain hunting in nearby villages and found lovely, simple pieces, such as this chair. The floor lamp is by Rico Espinet, in the wall cabinet is the rope for the old school bell.

Linke Seite: Auf dem Bibliothekstisch sind Entwürfe von Espinet, Fundstücke und Zigarrenkisten zu einem Gesamtkunstwerk arrangiert.
Oben: Gleich zwei der insgesamt drei großen Klassenräume hat Espinet in Studios umfunktioniert. Das eine für die groben Arbeiten, das andere (Foto), um den Stücken den letzten Schliff zu geben.
Rechts: Vandalen hatten kräftig zugeschlagen, so daß von der Originaleinrichtung der Schule nichts übriggeblieben war. Deshalb erträdelte Heloisa Zero in den benachbarten Orten einfache Möbelstücke, wie diesen Stuhl. Die Stehlampe ist von Rico Espinet, im Wandschränkchen endet das Seil der alten Schulglocke.

Ci-dessus et page de droite: *Dans le séjour, le tableau d'ardoise d'origine est toujours là. La table et les chaises viennent des Puces, la lampe et la sculpture près de la porte sont l'œuvre d'Espinet. Les housses du canapé varient selon les humeurs des habitants et les saisons. Le petit tableau est un cadeau de l'artiste américain décédé Jean-Michel Basquiat à son ami Rico Espinet. Lampadaire d'Espinet, fauteuil en bois trouvé chez l'antiquaire.*

Above and facing page: *In the living room the original slate blackboard still hangs on the wall. Table and chairs are from the flea-market, lamp and sculpture beside the door are by Espinet, the sofa throws can be changed for seasonal, temperamental or whimsical reasons. The small picture is a present from the late American artist Jean-Michel Basquiat to his friend Rico Espinet. Floor lamp by Espinet, wooden armchair from an antique store.*

Oben und rechte Seite: *Im Wohnzimmer hängt noch immer die Originaltafel aus Schiefer an der Wand. Tisch und Stühle sind vom Flohmarkt, die Lampe und die Skulptur neben der Tür von Espinet. Die Kissen auf dem Sofa werden nach Lust, Laune und Jahreszeit gewechselt. Das kleine Gemälde ist ein Geschenk des befreundeten, mittlerweile verstorbenen amerikanischen Künstlers Jean-Michel Basquiat an Rico Espinet. Die Stehlampe ist von Espinet, der Holzsessel aus dem Antiquitätengeschäft.*

Il y a près de vingt ans, le banquier en investissements et sa femme, designer florale, achetèrent leur ferme en Nouvelle-Angleterre. Ils venaient souvent y passer le week-end et ne songeaient pas du tout à la transformer. Avant eux, la propriété construite en 1762 et délabrée de la manière la plus romantique, avait été habitée par la même famille durant huit générations. Il y a cinq ans, ils ont rencontré l'architecte d'intérieur, designer et décorateur new-yorkais John Saladino. Avec la propriétaire des lieux il a réussi le tour de force qui était de restaurer et de moderniser parfaitement la maison sans lui faire perdre son âme. Aidés des artisans de la région, ils ont utilisé des matériaux modernes en travaillant à l'ancienne. Et la propriétaire a même semé dans son jardin des fleurs qui s'y trouvaient déjà en 1762.

Investment Banker

Almost twenty years ago the New York investment banker and his wife, a floral designer, bought their farmhouse in New England. They often spent weekends here and in their wildest dreams they never thought of remodeling. Before them, eight generations of the same family had lived in this romantically mellowed house, built in 1762. Five years ago they met the New York interior architect, designer and decorator John Saladino. Together with the owners he succeeded in restoring and modernizing the home perfectly and without harm to its centuries-old soul. He worked with local craftsmen, using old building techniques but modern materials. The owners even planted the garden with flower varieties that already existed in 1762.

Vor fast 20 Jahren kauften der New Yorker Investment-Banker und seine Frau, eine Blumen-Designerin, ihr Farmhaus in New England, kamen oft übers Wochenende und dachten im Traum nicht daran, es zu verändern. 1762 erbaut, hatten vorher acht Generationen derselben Familie in diesem aufs romantischste verwohnten Anwesen gelebt. Vor fünf Jahren trafen sie den New Yorker Innenarchitekten, Designer und Dekorateur John Saladino. Gemeinsam mit der Hausbesitzerin ist ihm das Kunststück gelungen, dem perfekt restaurierten und modernisierten Haus seine jahrhundertealte Seele zu belassen. Mit lokalen Handwerkern wurde nach alten Bauweisen mit modernen Materialien gearbeitet. Und die Besitzerin legte den Garten sogar mit Blumen an, die es auch 1762 schon gegeben hat.

Page précédente: Construite en 1762, la maison de campagne est un exemple parfait du style colonial de la Nouvelle-Angleterre. Dans la resserre à côté de la cuisine, comme dans toute la maison, le temps semble figé. D'ici on a accès à un jardin potager romantique.
Ci-dessus: Dans chaque pièce se trouvent une cheminée et quelques pièces de la vaste collection de chaises du maître de céans.
Page de droite: Là où c'était possible, l'architecte d'intérieur John Saladino a remis à nu les anciens murs de brique, ou – comme ici dans le grand salon/salle à manger, il a construit une cheminée en briques neuves, simulant parfaitement le travail ancien.

Vorhergehende Seite: 1762 erbaut, ist das Landhaus ein perfektes Beispiel des New-England-Colonial-Stils. Überall, wie hier im Vorratsraum neben der Küche scheint die Zeit stehengeblieben zu sein. Von hier aus gelangt man in einen romantischen Kräutergarten.
Oben: In jedem Wohnraum befinden sich ein Kamin und Teile der umfangreichen Stuhlsammlung der Hausbesitzer.
Rechte Seite: Wo möglich, hat Innenarchitekt John Saladino die alten Ziegelmauern wieder freigelegt oder – wie hier im großen Wohn- und Eßzimmer – aus neuen Ziegelsteinen einen Kamin gebaut, eine perfekte Simulation alter Bauweise.

Previous page: Built in 1762, the country house is a perfect example of the New England colonial style. Here in the modest storage room next to the kitchen, as everywhere in the house, time seems to have stood still. The storage room leads to the romantic herb garden.
Above: Every living room has a fireplace and a display of pieces from the owners' extensive chair collection.
Facing page: Wherever possible, interior architect John Saladino has exposed the old brick walls, or, as here in the large living and dining room, has built a fireplace with new bricks in a perfect simulation of old building methods.

Ci-dessus: La grande cuisine est équipée de manière ultramoderne sans perdre pour cela son caractère rustique.
A droite et page de droite: Pour dégager la vue superbe sur le fleuve, un pan de mur a été abattu et remplacé par une paroi largement vitrée. Des portes de verre s'ouvrent sur la prairie. Table de style shaker. Le canapé a été dessiné par John Saladino.

Above: The spacious kitchen has ultramodern equipment and yet still maintains its rural character.
Right and facing page: To pbtain the wonderful view of the nearby river, an entire wall was taken down at the front of the house and rebuilt as a window wall. Glass doors open to the meadow. The dining room has a Shaker-style table. The sofa is a design by John Saladino.

Oben: Die große Küche ist ultramodern eingerichtet und hat dennoch ihren ländlichen Charakter behalten.
Rechts und rechte Seite: Für den phantastischen Blick auf den nahen Fluß wurde eine gesamte Hausfront abgetragen und als Fensterfront wieder aufgebaut. Glastüren öffnen sich zur Wiese. Eßtisch im Shaker-Stil. Das Sofa ist ein Entwurf von John Saladino.

Page de gauche et ci-dessus: Chaque chambre à coucher possède sa propre grande cheminée. Ici, une chambre d'invités dans les tons cannelle. Sur la cheminée, un nid d'oiseau, que la propriétaire a trouvé abandonné dans le jardin. Les lits en cerisier, de style shaker, ont été fabriqués par un menuisier de la région.

Facing page and above: Each bedroom has its own large fireplace. The guest room here is painted in cinnamon color. On the fireplace is a bird's nest the owners found abandoned in the garden. The Shaker-style beds were newly built of cherry wood by a local cabinet-maker.

Linke Seite und oben: Jedes Schlafzimmer hat seinen eigenen großen Kamin. Hier ein zimtfarben gestrichenes Gästezimmer. Auf dem Kamin ein Vogelnest, das die Hausbesitzerin verlassen im Garten fand. Die Betten im Shaker-Stil sind neu und von einem lokalen Schreiner aus Kirschholz angefertigt worden.

Alexander Julian est designer de mode et connu pour la grande har-
diesse avec laquelle il manie les couleurs. Il a habillé des équipes entières de base-ball et aménagé en couleurs tout un stade, le «Knights
Castle» de Charlotte. Bill Clinton, Paul Newman, Michael J. Fox et
Harry Connick jr. aiment ce qu'il fait. Et évidemment, sa ligne de
maison qui comporte aussi bien le lit que les draps et taies, la vais-
selle que les torchons, est sous le signe de la couleur. Mais son chef-
d'œuvre, c'est sa maison de campagne au Connecticut où il vit avec
sa femme Meagan et ses quatre enfants, une maison de rêve que
Julian a conçue avec l'architecte californien John Marsh Davis. Un
arc-en-ciel de 56 couleurs, créées spécialement par Don Kaufman et
Taffy Dahl, des coloristes new-yorkais, enlumine la maison. Un
endroit où il fait bon vivre. Alexander Julian ne se contente pas de
mettre ses idées en pratique chez lui. Créateur d'une «Fondation pour
l'apprentissage esthétique», il s'efforce entre autres d'élaborer de
nouvelles méthodes pour développer la créativité enfantine.

Alexander Julian

Alexander Julian is a fashion designer, known for his bold use of
lively colors. He has done baseball uniforms and created the color
scheme of an entire stadium, "Knights Castle" in Charlotte, North
Carolina. Bill Clinton, Paul Newman, Michael J. Fox and Harry
Connick, Jr. love his fashions and, of course, his entire multicolored
home collection, from beds to bedsheets, dishes to dishtowels. But
his masterwork is his country house in Connecticut, where he lives
with his wife Meagan and four children. Designed by Julian and
the California architect John Marsh Davis, the house is a fanfare of
different shades of color, specially mixed by New York color experts
Don Kaufman and Taffy Dahl. It's a place of delight. In fact, as head
of the "Foundation for Aesthetic Learning", Alexander Julian is
especially concerned with new methods of furthering creativity in
children.

Alexander Julian ist Modedesigner und bekannt für seinen selbstbe-
wußten Umgang mit fröhlichen Farben. Er hat Baseballteams einge-
kleidet und ein ganzes Stadion, das »Knights Castle« in Charlotte,
farbig gestaltet. Seine Mode wird geliebt von Bill Clinton und Paul
Newman, von Michael J. Fox und Harry Connick jr. Und selbstverständlich ist auch seine Homecollection buntschillernd, vom Bett bis
zur Bettwäsche, vom Geschirr bis zum Geschirrtuch. Sein Meister-
werk ist das Landhaus in Connecticut, wo er mit seiner Frau Meagan
und den vier Kindern lebt – ein Traumhaus, das Julian mit dem
kalifornischen Architekten John Marsh Davis entworfen hat. Wie ein
Regenbogen durchfluten 56 verschiedene Farbtöne das Haus, die
eigens von den New Yorker Farbexperten Don Kaufman und Taffy
Dahl gemischt wurden. Ein Ort des Glücks. Alexander Julian macht
mit diesem Anspruch nicht hinter der eigenen Haustür Halt. Mit
der »Stiftung für ästhetisches Lernen« bemüht er sich unter anderem
um neue Methoden der Kreativitätsförderung von Kindern.

Premières pages: paysage de livre d'images au Connecticut: une pas-serelle romantique, un petit lac, et, au fond, la maison du designer de mode Alexander Julian qui vit ici avec son épouse et quatre enfants. Des poutres en acajou et des colonnes structurent le salon qui fait 7 m de haut. Au-dessus de la cheminée, un tableau de Tom Holland.
Double page précédente: un jeu fantastique avec les couleurs. La cage d'escalier en acajou n'en offre pas moins de dix. 56 tonalités différentes ont été utilisées dans l'ensemble de la maison, soigneuse-ment harmonisées entre elles par Alexander Julian et Don Kaufman, un spécialiste new-yorkais.
Ci-dessus: Dans la salle à manger, les chaises habillées de box multi-colore ont été conçues par Alexander Julian; son épouse Meagan a dessiné la table et les appliques. Parquet d'acajou.

First pages: a picture-book landscape in Connecticut: a romantic foot bridge, a small lake, in the background the country house of fashion designer Alexander Julian, where he lives with his wife Meagan and four children. Mahogany beams and columns define the interior of the almost 7 m high salon. Above the fireplace is a picture by Tom Holland.
Previous pages: fantastic play with colors. Ten shades can be detected in the mahogany stairwell alone. A total of 56 different tones were used in the country house, carefully coordinated by Alexander Julian and Don Kaufman, a New York color specialist.
Above: The colorful calfskin chairs in the dining room are by Alexan-der Julian, table and wall lamps were designed by his wife, Meagan. The floor is made of mahogany.

Erste Seiten: eine Bilderbuchlandschaft in Connecticut: ein romanti-scher Steg, ein kleiner See, dahinter das Landhaus von Modedesigner Alexander Julian, der hier mit seiner Frau Meagan und den vier Kin-dern lebt. Mahagonibalken und -stützen formen den Körper des 7 m hohen Salons. Über dem Kamin hängt ein Gemälde von Tom Holland.
Vorhergehende Doppelseite: phantastisches Spiel mit Farben: allein im Treppenhaus aus Mahagoniholz zählt man zehn. Insgesamt sind in dem Landhaus 56 verschiedene Farbtöne verwendet worden, die von Alexander Julian und Don Kaufman, einem New Yorker Farb-spezialisten, sorgfältig aufeinander abgestimmt wurden.
Oben: Die bunten kalbslederbezogenen Stühle im Eßzimmer hat Alexander Julian, den Tisch und die Wandleuchten seine Frau Meagan entworfen. Der Fußboden ist aus Mahagoniholz.

La bonne vieille cuisine de ferme américaine revue et corrigée. Elle s'ouvre sur la salle à manger. La table est en cerisier. Selon Meagan Julian, la cuisine a la couleur du risotto quand on y ajoute du safran.

The perfect example of an old American farmhouse kitchen. The room opens to the dining room. The work table is cherry wood. According to Meagan Julian, the color of the kitchen is saffron stirred into risotto.

Die perfektionierte Version einer alten amerikanischen Farmhaus-küche. Der Raum öffnet sich zum Eßzimmer. Der Arbeitstisch ist aus Kirschholz. Die Farbe der Küche entspricht, so Meagan Julian, dem Ton von Safran, wenn man das Gewürz in ein Risotto hineinrührt.

Page de gauche: Les parquets et les plafonds des chambres sont en
pin. Le lit de maître est d'Alexandre Julian, le manteau de cheminée
en céramique de Connie Leslie.
Ci-dessus: De la baignoire en fonte non encastrée, on a une belle vue
sur le paysage. L'armoire à linge en pin est peinte à la main, les ser-
viettes sont suspendues à un ancien étal de marché.

Facing page: Floors and ceilings in the sleeping area are panelled in
pine. The master bed was designed by Alexander Julian, the ceramic
fireplace is by Connie Leslie.
Above: The bath features a cast-iron tub with a view of the landscape. The Scotch pine linen closet is handpainted, the towels are
draped over an old stand from a market.

Linke Seite: Im Schlafbereich sind Böden und Decken mit Kiefernholz verkleidet. Das Bett ist ein Entwurf von Alexander Julian, der
Keramikkamin ist von Connie Leslie.
Oben: Von der freistehenden gußeisernen Badewanne hat man einen
schönen Blick auf die Landschaft. Der Wäscheschrank aus Kiefernholz
ist handbemalt, die Handtücher hängen über einem alten Markt-
stand.

Gael et Michael Mendelsohn vivent près de l'Hudson sur le plus ancien terrain de golf privé d'Amérique du Nord. La maison de 1000 m²
qui comprend sept pièces est un musée privé à la gloire de l'art popu-
laire américain. Gael Mendelsohn préserve avec beaucoup d'engage-
ment le «self-taught outsider folk art», l'art naïf américain contemporain, tableaux, sculptures, objets. Les autres collections sont tout
aussi remarquables: instruments de musique du 19e siècle finissant
et du début du 20e, guitares, banjos, concertinas, violons, saxophones
et keyboards, tambourins, grelots; des cannes artistement ciselées:
des «Anniversary Tins», ces objets d'étain que l'on offrait autrefois
à l'occasion des anniversaires «ronds»; des têtes de totems; des
«lunchboxes». Un jour, le maître de maison apporta une œuvre
volumineuse de Thornton Dial Sr. et constata qu'il ne pouvait la
placer nulle part. Très sérieusement, il demanda alors à sa femme:
«Avons-nous vraiment besoin de la porte d'entrée?»

Gael and Michael Mendelsohn

Gael and Michael Mendelsohn live by the Hudson River on the
oldest private golf course in North America. The 1000 sq.m.
seven-room house is a private museum of American folk art.
Gael Mendelsohn is dedicated to the preservation of "self-taught
outsider folk art", contemporary naive art, pictures, sculptures,
and objects. Equally remarkable are her other collections: musical
instruments from the turn of the century, guitars, banjos, concertinas, violins, saxophones, as well as keyboards, tambourines,
chimes, artfully carved walking sticks, "anniversary tins", totem
heads and lunchboxes. The master of the house came home one
day with an exceptionally large work by Thornton Dial Sr. and
realized that there was no room left for it anywhere. He looked
around and, quite seriously, asked his wife: "What do we need the
front door for?"

Gael und Michael Mendelsohn leben am Hudson River auf dem älte-
sten privaten Golfplatz Nordamerikas. Das 1000 m² große Haus mit
sieben Zimmern ist ein privates Museum amerikanischer Volkskunst.
Gael Mendelsohn ist eine engagierte Bewahrerin von »Self-taught
Outsider Folk Art«, zeitgenössischer Naiver Kunst, die mit Gemälden,
Skulpturen und anderen Objekten vertreten ist. Ebenso beachtlich
sind die weiteren Sammlungen: Musikinstrumente des ausgehenden
19. und beginnenden 20. Jahrhunderts, Gitarren, Banjos, Concertinas,
Geigen, Saxophone und Keyboards, Tamborine, Schellen. Außerdem
kunstvoll geschnitzte Spazierstöcke und »Anniversary Tins«, Zinn-
objekte, die man sich um die Jahrhundertwende zu runden Geburts-
tagen schenkte, und schließlich Totemköpfe und »Lunchboxes«. Eines
Tages kam der Hausherr mit einem besonders großen Werk von
Thornton Dial sr. nach Hause und stellte fest, daß es nirgendwo mehr
Platz dafür gab – alle Wände waren besetzt. Er sah sich um und
fragte seine Frau durchaus ernsthaft: »Wozu brauchen wir eigentlich
die Haustür?«

Ci-dessus: art utilitaire dans la cuisine: des «lunchboxes», les boîtes gaiement colorées qui contenaient le déjeuner des écoliers. Les boule-dogues anglais semblent bien massifs à côté de ces objets délicats.
Détail de la photo de gauche: sur le rebord de la fenêtre du séjour quelques «ragdolls» primées des années 30, des poupées de chiffon sudistes.

Above: functional art in the kitchen: colorful lunchboxes, for children to bring their lunch to school. The English bulldogs have the air of bulls in a china shop.
Detail photo left: In the living-room window are a few prize-winning ragdolls from the southern states, dating to the 30s.

Oben: Gebrauchskunst in der Küche: bunte »Lunchboxes«, in denen Kinder ihr Mittagessen mit zur Schule nahmen. Die englischen Bull-doggen wirken wie Elefanten im Porzellanladen.
Detailfoto links: Im Wohnzimmerfenster sind einige preisgekrönte Lumpenpuppen aus den Südstaaten der 30er Jahre dekoriert, soge-nannte »Ragdolls«.

*En haut à gauche, une partie de la collection d'instruments de
musique américains de la fin du 19e et du début du 20e siècle.
A droite, au-dessus de l'ancienne armoire d'épicier et près de la porte,
des tableaux de peintres naïfs américains contemporains.*

*Left, part of the American musical instrument collection from the late
19th and early 20th centuries. Above the old village-shop drawers and
around the door, works by contemporary American naive painters,
known as "outsiders".*

*Links ein Teil der Sammlung amerikanischer Musikinstrumente aus
dem späten 19. und frühen 20. Jahrhundert. Über dem alten Kauf-
ladenschrank und an der Tür Bilder zeitgenössischer amerikanischer
Naiver Maler, »Outsider« genannt.*

New York Interiors   Gael and Michael Mendelsohn

De gauche à droite et de haut en bas: la collection d'instruments de musique américains. Un fauteuil aux couleurs du drapeau américain réalisé par un artiste inconnu du tournant du siècle. Dans la chambre à coucher, une commode de Cortland/New York, 1880, chaque tiroir est décoré d'un paysage différent. Gael Mendelsohn a déniché le taureau sculpté dans une grange des Etats du Sud, la sculpture en bois est de Raymond Coins et l'une des premières pièces de la collection d'art «outsider» des Mendelsohn. Dans la salle de bains, des masques rituels guatemaltèques, mexicains et africains.

Clockwise from top left: A collection of American musical instruments. Next, an armchair, painted red, white and blue, by an anonymous turn-of-the-century painter. In the bedroom a chest from Cortland, New York, 1880. Each drawer is painted with a different landscape. Gael Mendelsohn dug up the bull sculpture in a barn in the South. The wooden figure is by Raymond Coins and was one of the first pieces in the Mendelsohn collection of outsider art. In the bathroom are ritual masks from Guatemala, Mexico and Africa.

Im Uhrzeigersinn von links oben: die Sammlung amerikanischer Musikinstrumente. Ein in den amerikanischen Farben bemalter Sessel von einem unbekannten Künstler der Jahrhundertwende. Im Schlafzimmer eine Kommode aus Cortland, New York, von 1880. Jede Schublade ist mit einer anderen Landschaft bemalt. Die Stierskulptur hat Gael Mendelsohn in einer Scheune in den Südstaaten aufgestöbert. Die Holzfigur von Raymond Coins ist eines der ersten Stücke der Sammlung von Outsider-Kunst. Im Bad hängen Ritualmasken aus Guatemala, Mexiko und Afrika.

Le réalisateur Steven Spielberg, dont les films ont battu les records du plus grand nombre d'entrées, a déjà construit au début des années 80 la première partie de sa propriété de East Hampton à Long Island, qui comprend aujourd'hui trois grands bâtiments. Une vieille grange, «Quelle Barn» que l'équipe d'architectes Gwathmey/Siegel fit transporter de Pennsylvanie, fut la première installée, puis vint la maison principale (nos photos) et, il y a cinq ans, un vaste complexe pour les invités. Situé au milieu d'un doux paysage de prairies, le village de Spielberg est une retraite pour sa grande famille et les nombreux invités. Construites dans le style New Modernism, les fermes ultramodernes revêtues de lattes de bois s'adaptent parfaitement à l'environnement. L'ameublement est simple et fonctionnel; on fait fi des chichis quand on a cinq enfants. On cherche vainement des objets design; l'architecte d'intérieur Naomi Leff a réuni du bon artisanat américain. Les Spielberg passent ici une grande partie de l'été.

Steven Spielberg

In the early 80s, Steven Spielberg, Oscar winner and the most successful film director of all times, built the first structure on his East Hampton estate on Long Island, which today includes three houses. First came the old "Quelle Barn", brought here from Pennsylvania by the architect team Gwathmey/Siegel, then the main house (our photos) and, five years ago, an elaborate guest complex. Amidst meadows in a flat landscape, not visible from the road, the Spielberg village is a refuge for his large family and many guests. Built in New Modernism style, the ultramodern shigled farmhouses fit in perfectly with their surroundings. The furnishings are functional and simple; with five children there is no need for frills. For the interior design Naomi Leff has relied largely on pieces of solid American craftsmanship. The Spielbergs stay here for a good part of the summer.

Schon Anfang der 80er Jahre baute sich Steven Spielberg, Oscar-Preisträger und erfolgreichster Filmregisseur aller Zeiten, den ersten Teil seines heute drei große Häuser umfassenden Landsitzes in East Hampton auf Long Island. Zuerst wurde eine alte Scheune, »Quelle Barn« genannt, vom Architektenteam Gwathmey/Siegel aus Pennsylvania hierher transportiert, dann wurden das Haupthaus (unsere Fotos) und vor fünf Jahren noch ein großzügiger Gästekomplex errichtet. Inmitten einer flachen Wiesenlandschaft und von der Straße aus nicht einsehbar ist das Spielberg-Dorf Refugium für seine große Familie und die vielen Gäste. Im New-Modernism-Stil gebaut fügen sich die ultramodernen, mit Holzschindeln verkleideten Farmhäuser perfekt in die Umgebung ein. Die Einrichtung ist funktionell und einfach – bei fünf Kindern wird auf Schnickschnack gern verzichtet. Design fehlt fast ganz, dafür hat Interior-Designerin Naomi Leff gutes amerikanisches Kunsthandwerk zusammengetragen. Die Spielbergs verbringen hier einen großen Teil des Sommers.

Page précédente: ambiance crépusculaire: la maison de campagne revêtue d'un bardage de bois est située à East Hampton, Long Island. Les architectes new-yorkais Gwathmey Siegel l'ont conçue pour le réalisateur Steven Spielberg, son épouse Kate Capeshaw et leurs cinq enfants.

Ci-dessus et page de droite: Jeux de lumière dans la vaste entrée avec ses cages d'escalier symétriques qui mènent aux galeries et aux chambres à coucher. Spielberg – et l'architecte d'intérieur Naomi Leff avec qui il a collaboré pour aménager ses habitations – ne fait pas grand cas de meubles de designers ou d'antiquités venues d'Europe. Il apprécie le bon artisanat américain, Arts and Crafts, dont de nombreuses pièces ont été réalisées spécialement pour cette maison.

Vorhergehende Seite: im Abendlicht: das mit Holzschindeln verkleidete Landhaus in East Hampton auf Long Island, das die New Yorker Architekten Gwathmey/Siegel für Oscar-Preisträger Steven Spielberg, seine Frau Kate Capeshaw und ihre fünf Kinder gebaut haben.

Oben und rechte Seite: Lichtspiele in dem großzügigen Eingangsbereich mit den symetrischen Treppenhäusern, die hinaufführen auf Galerien und in den Schlafbereich. Spielberg und die Interior-Designerin Naomi Leff, mit der er bei der Einrichtung all seiner Wohnsitze zusammengearbeitet hat, legen keinen Wert auf Designermöbel oder europäische Antiquitäten. Stattdessen auf gutes amerikanisches Kunsthandwerk, Arts and Crafts; viele Stücke wurden eigens für dieses Haus angefertigt.

Previous page: bathed in evening light, the shingle country home in East Hampton, Long Island, built by New York architects Gwathmey Siegel for Oscar winner Steven Spielberg, his wife Kate Capeshaw and their five children.

Above and facing page: Sunlight plays in the spacious entrance hall with its symmetrical staircases, which lead by way of galleries to the bedroom areas. Spielberg and his interior decorator Naomi Leff, who worked with him on all his residences, place little value on designer furniture or European antiques. Many pieces for the house were custom-made by good American artisans.

Pages suivantes: La salle de séjour au plafond haut de 7 m est dominée par de vieilles poutres brutes qui proviennent pour la plupart de Pennsylvanie. La cheminée et les escaliers génèrent des formes géométriques intéressantes. La façade vitrée offre une vue sublime sur le paysage égal d'East Hampton. La maison bénéficie de toutes les techniques modernes, subtilement intégrées dans l'ensemble, la climatisation et les mécanismes des fenêtres sont invisibles.

Following pages: Old roughhewn beams, many of them brought from Pennsylvania, dominate the 7 m high living room. The fireplace and stairs produce a fascinating interplay of geometric forms. The glass front offers a spectacular view over the vast East Hampton plains. Ingeniously installed, heating and air-conditioning systems, as well as window mechanisms, are completely invisible.

Folgende Seiten: Die 7 m hohe Wohnhalle wird dominiert von den alten rohen Balken, die größtenteils aus Pennsylvania stammen. Der Kamin bildet mit den Treppen interessante geometrische Formen. Die Glasfront bietet einen phantastischen Ausblick über die weite flache Landschaft von East Hampton. Raffiniert eingebaut ist die perfekte Technik: Klimaanlage und Fenstermechanismen bleiben unsichtbar.

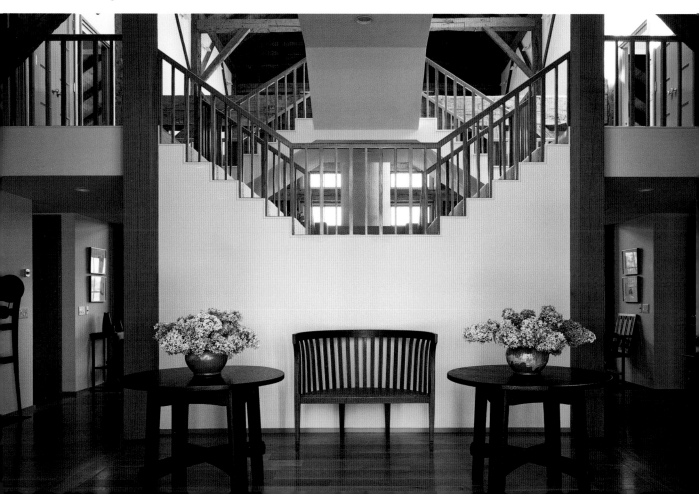

La chambre à coucher de Steven Spielberg et de son épouse. Sobre et confortable avec ses sièges blancs et son grand lit garni de coussins douillets et de draps de lin.

The bedroom of Steven Spielberg and his wife Kate Capeshaw. An oversize master bed with snuggle pillows and linen sheets, complemented by the white seating nook in the background.

Schlafzimmer von Steven Spielberg und seiner Frau Kate Capeshaw. Gemütlich wirken das große Bett mit Kuschelkissen, Leinenbettwäsche und die weiße Sitzecke.

C'est à Rhinebeck sur l'Hudson, au milieu d'un parc retourné à l'état sauvage, que se trouve Wilderstein, un des derniers authentiques châteaux victoriens d'Amérique. Margaret «Daisy» Lynch Suckley a vécu ici, seule à la fin, jusqu'à sa mort survenue récemment à l'âge de 99 ans. Construite en 1853 par son grand-père dans le style italien, modernisée par ses parents en 1888 dans le style Queen Anne, la propriété resta ensuite un voyage dans l'univers de styles exquis: entrée et salle à manger, début du 17e siècle anglais, dans le style Jacques Ier, bibliothèque Moyen Age flamand, salon-fumoir dans le style colonial américain, grand salon Louis XVI. Wilderstein n'a été rattaché au réseau d'électricité qu'en 1950, et la vieille dame ne s'est offert le luxe d'un téléviseur qu'au début des années 80. L'avenir de Wilderstein n'est pas encore fixé. La fondation qui gère la propriété veut en tout cas préserver l'esprit de la maison, ce mélange de permanence et de dégradation, de décadence et d'un charme fin de siècle à jamais enfui.

Margaret Lynch Suckley

In Rhinebeck on the Hudson River, in the midst of an overgrown park, stands Wilderstein, one of the last authentic Victorian mansions in America. Until her recent death at 99, Margaret "Daisy" Lynch Suckley lived in the Italianate house, built by her grandfather in 1853. After a Queen Anne "modernization" by her parents in 1888, the estate remained a journey around the world of exquisite styles. Entrance and dining room are early English 17th century, the library is medieval Flemish, the master's drawing room American Colonial, the large salon, Louis-XVI. Wilderstein remained without electricity until 1950, and only in the early 80s did Miss Lynch Suckley treat herself to a television set, which she only turned on to watch the world news. Though its future is uncertain, the noble spirit of Wilderstein will be preserved, as a witness to both stability and transience, but above all the charm of a bygone era.

In Rhinebeck am Hudson River liegt inmitten eines verwilderten Parks Wilderstein, eines der letzten authentischen viktorianischen Mansions Amerikas. Bis zu ihrem kürzlichen Tod mit 99 Jahren lebte hier Margaret »Daisy« Lynch Suckley – zuletzt allein. Von ihrem Großvater 1853 in italienischem Stil erbaut, von ihren Eltern 1888 im Queen-Anne-Stil »modernisiert«, blieb der Besitz seitdem eine Reise um die Welt erlesener Stile. Entrée und Speisezimmer im Stil des frühen englischen 17. Jahrhunderts, die Bibliothek in der Art des flämischen Mittelalters, das Herrenzimmer im amerikanischen Kolonialstil, der große Salon im Louis-XVI-Stil. Erst 1950 wurde Wilderstein mit Elektrizität ausgestattet, und erst Anfang der 80er Jahre gönnte sich die alte Dame einen Fernseher. Die Zukunft von Wilderstein ist momentan noch ungeklärt. Auf jeden Fall will die den Besitz verwaltende Stiftung den vornehmen Geist des Hauses erhalten: ein Potpourri aus Beständigkeit, Verfall, Dekadenz und Charme des vergangenen Fin de siècle.

Premières pages: Le salon Louis XVI a été restauré pour la dernière fois en 1888. Les colonnes, la cheminée et les plateaux de tables sont en onyx, les meubles et les stucs couleur or bruni. Les murs sont tendus de damas doré, en relativement bon état. La fresque «céleste» au plafond est de H. Siddons Mowbray, un artiste de l'époque.

Photos de détails: Sur le piano, une photo de Franklin D. Roosevelt, 1882–1945, 32e président des Etats-Unis et cousin de Miss Suckley. Elle travailla avec lui au cours des années 30 et lui offrit le célèbre terrier écossais Fala. Wilderstein a 35 pièces, une tourelle d'observation et une façade habillée de lattes de bois.

Double page précédente: Miss «Daisy» Suckley, qui a vu passer le siècle, dans le grand salon. Comme cinq de ses six frères et sœurs décédés depuis longtemps, elle est restée célibataire.

Ci-dessus et page de gauche: Autrefois on donnait des réceptions l'été dans la véranda. Aujourd'hui, des meubles de jardin en osier, une vieille voiture d'enfants et un fauteuil roulant sommeillent ici. Le parc de quarante arpents, où la nature a en grande partie repris ses droits, a été aménagé en 1891 par Downing & Vaux, les architectes paysagistes les plus renommés de l'époque qui ont eu aussi une contribution importante à la conception de Central Park.

First pages: The Louis XVI salon saw its last renovation in 1888. Columns, fireplace and table tops are of onyx, furniture and stucco bronze-gilded. The walls are covered with golden damask, threadbare only in places. The ceiling fresco with putti is by the contemporary artist H. Siddons Mowbray.

Detail photos: On the piano a photo of the 32nd president, Franklin D. Roosevelt (1882–1945), Miss Suckley's cousin. She worked with him in the 30s and gave him the famous Scotch terrier, Fala, as a present. Wilderstein has 35 rooms, a lookout tower and a wood-shingle façade.

Previous pages: Witness of an entire century: Miss "Daisy" Suckley, 99, in the grand salon. Like five of her six long since deceased siblings, she was never married.

Above and facing page: Summer receptions of long ago echo on the veranda, where wicker furniture, an old baby carriage and a wheel chair slumber. The 30 acre park, now grown wild, was laid out in 1891 by Downing & Vaux, the most renowned landscape architects of their time, who were also instrumental in the planning of Central Park.

Erste Seiten: Der Louis-XVI-Salon wurde 1888 zum letzten Mal renoviert. Säulen, Kamin und Tischplatten sind aus Onyx, Möbel und Stuck bronzevergoldet. Die Wände sind mit goldenem, nur teilweise verschlissenem Damast bespannt. Das Deckenfresko mit den Putten hat der zeitgenössische Künstler H. Siddons Mowbray gemalt.

Detailfotos: Auf dem Piano ein Foto des 32. amerikanischen Präsidenten Franklin D. Roosevelt (1882–1945), Miss Suckleys Cousin, mit dem sie in den 30er Jahren arbeitete und dem sie den berühmten Scotchterrier Fala schenkte. Wilderstein hat 35 Räume, einen Aussichtsturm und ist mit Holzschindeln verkleidet.

Vorhergehende Doppelseite: Zeugin eines ganzen Jahrhunderts: Miss »Daisy« Suckley, 99 Jahre, im großen Salon. Wie fünf ihrer sechs längst verstorbenen Geschwister war sie nie verheiratet.

Oben und rechte Seite: Auf der Veranda wurden früher Sommerempfänge gegeben. Heute schlummern hier Gartenmöbel aus Weidengeflecht, ein alter Kinderwagen und ein Rollstuhl. Der 40 Morgen große Park, heute größtenteils verwildert, wurde von Downing & Vaux 1891 angelegt, den damals renommiertesten Landschaftsarchitekten, die auch maßgeblich an der Planung des Central Park beteiligt waren.

Glossary / Glossar / Glossaire

Apartment

The first apartment houses in New York were built in 1870, which was a revolutionary development in housing for the increasing middle class, wanting to get away from the dark tenement houses. In 1870 Richard Morris Hunt built the Stevens House, the first apartment house with an elevator to transport people. The most famous apartment house in New York is the Dakota on Central Park West, built by Hardenbergh in 1880 with apartments containing up to 20 large rooms.

Die ersten Apartmenthäuser New Yorks wurden ab ca. 1870 erbaut, eine revolutionäre Wohnentwicklung der wachsenden Mittelklasse heraus aus den engen dunklen Reihenhäusern. Richard Morris Hunt erbaute 1870 das Stevens House mit dem ersten Personenaufzug in einem Wohngebäude. Berühmtestes Apartmenthaus New Yorks ist das 1880 von Hardenbergh erbaute Dakota Building am Central Park West, mit bis zu 20 Zimmern großen Wohnungen.

Les premiers immeubles d'appartements new-yorkais ont été édifiés à partir de 1870, une évolution révolutionnaire au sein des classes sociales moyennes qui quittent leurs maisons sombres et étroites en enfilade. Richard Morris Hunt construisit en 1870 la Stevens House, la première maison d'habitation à posséder un ascenseur. Les appartements les plus célèbres de New York se trouvent dans le Dakota Building édifié par Hardenbergh en 1880 à Central Park West. Ils ont parfois jusqu'à 20 pièces.

Beaux-Arts

A pompous New York building style influenced by the Paris Ecole des Beaux-Arts. Examples are the New York Public Library, Grand Central Station et al.

Von der Pariser Ecole des Beaux-Arts beeinflußter pompöser Baustil in New York, z. B. New York Public Library und Grand Central Station.

Bâtiments pompeux à New York, de style influencé par l'Ecole parisienne des Beaux-Arts, par exemple New York Public Library, Grand Central Station.

Brick

Dark red building blocks of molded clay in different standard sizes, often used for buildings in New York especially in the architecture of the late 19th century.

Dunkelroter Ziegelstein in verschiedenen Standardgrößen, bei New Yorker Bauten, besonders der Architektur des späten 19. Jahrhunderts, vielfach verwendet.

Briques rouge sombre existant en plusieurs tailles standard, souvent utilisées à New York, particulièrement dans les constructions du 19e siècle finissant.

Brownstone Building

Row houses, 3 to 4 floors high, of dark sandstone built in all parts of New York during the 19th century. Especially well preserved or restored examples in Greenwich Village, on the Upper West and Upper East Side, and on Riverside Drive.

Zwei- bis dreigeschossige Reihenwohnhäuser aus dunklem Sandstein. In allen Stadtteilen New Yorks während des 19. Jahrhunderts erbaut. Besonders gut erhaltene oder restaurierte Bauten in Greenwich Village, Upper West und Upper East Side, Riverside Drive.

Maisons en enfilade de 2 à 3 étages en grès de couleur sombre. Construites dans tous les quartiers de New York au 19e siècle. Particulièrement bien conservées ou restaurées à Greenwich Village, Upper West et Upper East Side, Riverside Drive.

Cast-Iron

Until around 1880, before the advent of steel, iron was used as building material and molded into various forms and decorative work in filigree. Beautiful examples are in TriBeCa and SoHo, such as the Gunther Building, 72 Greene Street, corner of Broome Street, or some subway station entrances.

Vor Stahl wurde in verschiedenste Formen gegossenes filigran dekoratives Eisen bis ca. 1880 als Baumaterial häufig verwendet. Schöne Beispiele in TriBeCa und SoHo, z. B. das Gunther Building, 72 Greene Street, Ecke Broome Street, oder etliche Eingänge zu den Subway Stations.

Jusque vers 1880, avant l'apparition de l'acier, le fer travaillé aux formes décoratives et délicates était un matériau de construction apprécié. De beaux exemples à TriBeCa et SoHo, par exemple le Gunther Building, 72 Greene Street au coin de la Broome Street, et de nombreuses bouches de métro.

Classical Revival, Gothic Revival, Neo-Renaissance

Revival and imitation of classical architecture and building styles of various European epochs, for instance of antiquity or the Gothic period.

Wiederaufleben und Nachahmung der klassischen Architektur und Baustile verschiedenster europäischer Epochen, z. B. der Antike und der Gotik.

Renaissance et imitation de l'architecture classique et des styles européens de diverses époques, antique ou gothique par exemple.

Decorative Arts

New York was the center for the design and production of furniture made in the colonial style of the 17th century, which started off a major innovative furniture industry. In American interior design today, the colonial style is often seen copied and refined.

New York war das Zentrum für Entwurf und Herstellung von Möbeln im Kolonialstil des 17. Jahrhunderts. Daraus entwickelte sich eine innovative Möbelindustrie, die sich heute im amerikanischen Interior Design vielfach kopiert und verfeinert wiederfindet.

New York était le centre de la conception et de la fabrication de meubles de style colonial du 17e siècle. Sur cette base s'est développée une industrie du meuble très variée et innovante, que l'on retrouve aujourd'hui souvent copiée et affinée dans la décoration d'intérieurs américaine.

Limestone

Milliennia old sandstone from the sea, made up of sand and seashells, soft and easy to work with. Extensively used as interior and exterior building material.

Am Meer gewonnener jahrtausende alter Sandstein, gepreßt aus Sand und Muscheln, weich und leicht zu verarbeiten. Häufig verwendeter Baustoff, innen und außen.

Il s'agit d'une pierre calcaire millénaire que l'on trouve en bord de mer. Faite de sable et de coquillages, elle est tendre et facile à travailler. Matériau de construction souvent utilisé à l'intérieur et à l'extérieur.

Loft

The original name for industrial buildings several floors high, built in Lower Manhattan, mostly between 1870 and 1930. Since the 70s more and more of these early factory halls were rebuilt into apartments and studios; a loft now means a large apartment without the traditional room division, in principle a gigantic, high room, having several functions.

Ursprünglich Bezeichnung für mehrstöckige Industriegebäude, z. B. in Lower Manhattan, die meist zwischen 1870 und 1930 erbaut wurden. Seit den 70er Jahren immer mehr dieser Fabrikhallen zu Wohn- und Studiozwecken umgebaut wurden, bezeichnet man als Loft mittlerweile jede großzügige Wohnung, die auf die traditionelle Raumaufteilung verzichtet und aus einem riesigen, hohen, multifunktionalen Raum besteht.

A l'origine, le terme désignait les locaux industriels de plusieurs étages, à Lower Manhattan par exemple, construits le plus souvent entre 1870 et 1930. Depuis le début des années 70, de plus en plus de ces anciennes usines ont été transformées en habitations et en studios, et on appelle maintenant loft tout appartement de vastes dimensions qui renonce à la répartition traditionnelle des pièces. Il ne comporte en principe qu'un espace polyvalent, gigantesque et au plafond élevé.

Mansion

City villas that resemble palaces, built for old New York families between the middle and the end of the 19th century on Park Avenue and Broadway for instance, later often torn down to make room for new apartment houses. Some have been preserved, such as the Frick Museum opposite Central Park between East 70th and 71st Street.

Mitte bis Ende des 19. Jahrhunderts erbaute palastartige Stadtvillen der alten New Yorker Familien, z. B. an der Park Avenue und auf dem Broadway, die später oft zugunsten von Neubauten von Apartmenthäusern abgerissen wurden. Einige sind erhalten, z. B. das heutige Frick Museum am Central Park zwischen East 70th und 71st Street.

Demeures citadines aux allures de palais construites par les vieilles familles new-yorkaises du milieu à la fin du 19e siècle, par exemple sur la Park Avenue et à Broadway. Avec le temps, elles ont souvent dû céder la place à de nouveaux immeubles d'appartements. Il en subsiste quelques-unes, par exemple le Frick Museum en face de Central Park entre East 70th et 71st Street.

Skyscraper

The first "skyscraper" in New York was the Equitable Building with 7½ floors, built in 1868. It was the first office building that had an elevator. Today 25 of the 100 highest buildings in the world are still found in New York, such as the famous Empire State Building, 381 m high.

Der erste »Wolkenkratzer« New Yorks war das 1868 erbaute Equitable Building mit 7½ Stockwerken, das erste Bürogebäude, das einen Aufzug hatte. Heute befinden sich in New York immer noch 25 der 100 höchsten Gebäude der Welt, unter anderen das berühmte 381 m hohe Empire State Building.

Le premier «gratte-ciel» de New York a été construit en 1868. Il s'agit du Equitable Building de 7½ étages, le premier immeuble de bureaux doté d'un ascenseur. Aujourd'hui, New York possède toujours 25 des 100 bâtiments les plus élevés du monde, entre autres le célèbre Empire State Building qui fait 381 m de haut.

Sliver Building

In the 70s and 80s with the price explosion for a square foot of land, especially on the Upper East Side, a few buildings were built up to 30 floors high and extremely narrow, with only one single apartment on each floor. One such building is on 350 East 86th Street, another on 266 East 78th Street.

Im Zuge der explodierenden Bodenpreise, besonders in der Upper East Side, wurden in den 70er und 80er Jahren etliche bis zu 30 Stockwerke hohe extrem schmale Apartmenthäuser erbaut, die pro Stockwerk jeweils nur eine einzige Wohnung hatten, z. B. 350 East 86th Street oder 266 East 78th Street.

L'explosion des prix du terrain à bâtir, particulièrement dans la Upper East Side, a entraîné au cours des années 70 et 80 la construction de nombreux immeubles d'appartements étroits et comptant jusqu'à 30 étages, chacun n'abritant qu'un appartement. Exemples: 350 East 86th ou 266 East 78th Street.

Town House

Splendid town houses were built for wealthy New Yorkers especially on the Upper West Side and the Upper East Side, for the most part in the middle of the 19th century up to the turn of the century.

Prachtvolle Stadthäuser wohlhabender New Yorker vornehmlich in der Upper West und Upper East Side, meist Mitte des 19. Jahrhunderts bis zur Jahrhundertwende erbaut.

Somptueuses résidences urbaines des New-Yorkais prospères, situées surtout Upper West et Upper East Side, construites le plus souvent du milieu du 19e jusqu'au tournant du siècle.

Notable Historic Buildings in Manhattan (selection, from Downtown to Uptown)
Bemerkenswerte historische Wohnhäuser in Manhattan (Auswahl, von Downtown nach Uptown)
Remarquables maisons d'habitation historiques à Manhattan (sélection, de Downtown à Uptown)

Puck Building
295–307 Lafayette Street/
Houston Street

Architect: Albert Wagner, built 1886/1893. Red brick; former publishing house of the satirical magazine "Puck", currently lofts.

Architekt: Albert Wagner, 1886/1893 erbaut. Rotes Backsteingebäude; früher Verlag des Satire-Magazins »Puck«, jetzt Lofts.

Architecte: Albert Wagner, construit en 1886/1893. Bâtiment de briques rouges; ancienne maison d'édition du magazine satirique «Puck», aujourd'hui lofts.

The Little Singer Building
561 Broadway/Spring Street

Architect: Ernest Flagg, built 1904. Cast iron and terracotta; window-construction became model for modern architecture of the 50s and 60s; former workshops of Singer Sewing Machines, currently offices and lofts.

Architekt: Ernest Flagg, 1904 erbaut. Cast-Iron und Terrakotta; Fensterkonstruktion als Vorbild für moderne Architektur der 50er und 60er Jahre; früher Werkstätten von Singer-Nähmaschinen, jetzt Büros und Lofts.

Architecte: Ernest Flagg, construit en 1904. Fonte et terre cuite; la construction des fenêtres est un modèle de l'architecture moderne des années 50 et 60; autrefois ateliers des machines à coudre Singer, aujourd'hui bureaux et lofts.

Haughwout Store
488 Broadway/Broome Street

Architect: John P. Gaynor, built 1857. Ironwork by Badger Iron Works; first Otis elevator in the world; former warehouse of porcelain dealer Eder V. Haughwout, currently lofts.

Architekt: John P. Gaynor, 1857 erbaut. Eisenarbeit von Badger Iron Works; erster Otis-Aufzug der Welt; früher Lagerhaus des Porzellanwarenhändlers Eder V. Haughwout, jetzt Lofts.

Architecte: John P. Gaynor, construit en 1857. Ferrures de Badger Iron Works; premier ascenseur Otis du monde; autrefois entrepôt du marchand de porcelaines Eder V. Haughwout, aujourd'hui lofts.

The Row
1–13 Washington Square North/
University Place and Fifth Avenue

Various architects, built 1832–1833. Splendid terraced houses, former apartments of well-to-do bankers and business people, later of intellectuals and artists such as Henry James and Edward Hopper.

Diverse Architekten, 1832–1833 erbaut. Prachtvolle Reihenhäuser, früher Wohnungen von vornehmen Bankern und Kaufleuten, später auch von Intellektuellen und Künstlern wie Henry James und Edward Hopper.

Divers architectes, construits en 1832–1833. Superbes maisons en enfilade, autrefois appartements de banquiers et commerçants distingués, plus tard aussi d'intellectuels et d'artistes comme Henry James et Edward Hopper.

Christadora House
1 Tompkins Square, 145 Avenue B

Architect: Henry C. Pelton, built 1928. Tile and sandstone in a stylistic mixture of neoclassical and Art Deco. George Gershwin gave his first concert in the ballroom; today studios and apartments.

Architekt: Henry C. Pelton, 1928 erbaut. Ziegel und Sandstein im Stilmix des Neoklassizismus und Art Déco. Im Ballsaal gab George Gershwin sein erstes Konzert; heute Ateliers und Apartments.

Architecte: Henry C. Pelton, construite en 1928. Briques et grès, mélange de styles néoclassique et Art Déco. George Gershwin donna son premier concert dans la salle de bal; aujourd'hui ateliers et appartements.

Chelsea Hotel
222 West 23rd Street/
7th and 8th Avenue

Architect: Hubert, Piersson & Co, built 1884. Victorian Gothic with ornamental iron balconies. A hotel since 1905 with mostly permanent guests such as Mark Twain, Tennessee Williams, Arthur Miller and Jackson Pollock. Andy Warhol filmed "Chelsea Girls" here.

Architekt: Hubert, Piersson & Co, 1884 erbaut. Viktorianische Gotik mit ornamentalen Eisenbalkonen. Seit 1905 Hotel mit vornehmlich festen Bewohnern; hier lebten Mark Twain, Tennessee Williams, Arthur Miller, Jackson Pollock. Andy Warhol drehte hier seinen Film »Chelsea Girls«.

Architecte: Hubert, Piersson & Co, construit en 1884. Style gothique victorien avec balcons ornementaux de fer forgé. Depuis 1905, hôtel avec surtout des habitants fixes; Mark Twain, Tennessee Williams, Arthur Miller, Jackson Pollock y ont vécu. Andy Warhol a tourné ici son film «Chelsea Girls».

Alwyn Court
180 West 58th Street

Architect: Harde & Short, built 1909. French Renaissance-style façade complete with terracotta decor; in inner courtyard a fantastic mural by Richard Haas; apartments.

Architekt: Harde & Short, 1909 erbaut. Fassade im Stil der französischen Renaissance, komplett mit Terrakotta-Dekor überzogen; im Innenhof eine phantastische Fassadenmalerei von Richard Haas; Apartments.

Architecte: Harde & Short, construit en 1909. Façade dans le style de la Renaissance française, revêtu complètement d'un décor en terre cuite; peinture murale superbe de Richard Haas dans la cour intérieure; appartements.

Ansonia Hotel
2109 Broadway/West 73rd and
West 74th Street

Architect: Graves & Duboy, built 1904 in the grand Parisian manner of a palatial apartment building. Amongst those who stayed here were Arturo Toscanini and Igor Stravinsky.

Architekt: Graves & Duboy, 1904 erbaut. Im Stil hochherrschaftlicher Pariser Apartmenthäuser; unter anderen lebten hier Arturo Toscanini und Igor Strawinsky.

Architecte: Graves & Duboy, construit en 1904. Style des maisons de maître parisiennes; ont vécu ici entre autres Arturo Toscanini et Igor Stravinsky.

The Dakota Building
1 West 72nd Street/
Central Park West

Architect: Henry J. Hardenbergh, built 1884. First luxury apartment building in Manhattan, built for Edward J. Clark the heir of Singer Sewing Machines. Roman Polanski filmed "Rosemary's Baby" here and John Lennon was murdered in front of the house.

Architekt: Henry J. Hardenbergh, 1884 erbaut. Erstes luxuriöses Apartmenthaus Manhattans, erbaut für Edward S. Clark, den Erben der Singer-Nähmaschinenwerke. Roman Polanski drehte hier »Rosemary's Baby«, Leonard Bernstein lebte hier, und John Lennon, der auf der Straße vor dem Haus ermordet wurde.

Architecte: Henry J. Hardenbergh, construit en 1884. Premier immeuble d'appartements luxueux de Manhattan, bâti pour Edward S. Clark, l'héritier des machines à coudre Singer. Roman Polanski a tourné ici «Rosemary's Baby», Leonard Bernstein y a vécu, ainsi que John Lennon, qui a trouvé la mort dans la rue devant la maison.

The Langham
135 Central Park West/
West 73rd and West 74th Street

Architect: Clinton & Russell built 1905. Beaux-art style with fantastic façade; luxury apartments.

Architekt: Clinton & Russell, 1905 erbaut. Beaux-Art-Stil mit phantastischer Fassade; Luxus-Apartments.

Architecte: Clinton & Russell, construit en 1905. Style Beaux-Arts, façade sublime; appartements de luxe.

San Remo
145–146 Central Park West/
West 74th and West 75th Street

Architect: Emery Roth, built 1930. Two palatial tower blocks which look like Roman temples in the sky; luxury apartments.

Architekt: Emery Roth, 1930 erbaut. Zwei palastartige Wohntürme, die wie in den Himmel gemalte römische Tempel wirken; Luxus-Apartments.

Architecte: Emery Roth, construit en 1930. Deux tours d'habitation somptueuses, qui ressemblent à des temples romains peints dans le ciel; appartements de luxe.

The Studio Building
44 West 77th Street/
Central Park West

Architect: Harde & Short, built 1909. Neo-Gothic terracotta façade; studio apartments with north light.

Architekt: Harde & Short, 1909 erbaut. Neogotische Terrakotta-Fassade; Wohnateliers mit Nordlicht.

Architecte: Harde & Short, construit en 1909. Façade néogothique aux décorations de terre cuite; maisons-ateliers éclairées du nord.

Sherry Netherland Hotel
781 Fifth Avenue/East 59th Street

Architect: Schulze & Weaver, built 1927. Elegant hotel and apartment building with crowning minaret on roof.

Architekt: Schulze & Weaver, 1927 erbaut. Elegantes Hotel- und Apartmentgebäude mit minarettartiger Dachkrone.

Architecte: Schulze & Weaver, construit en 1927. Elégant hôtel et immeuble d'appartements avec corniche en forme de minaret.

The Pierre
795 Fifth Avenue/East 61st Street

Architect: Schulze & Weaver, built 1929. Narrow elegant hotel and apartment building; the ballroom on the top floor is now a private luxury aparment.

Architekt: Schulze & Weaver, 1929 erbaut. Schmales, elegantes Hotel- und Apartmentgebäude; der Ballsaal im Dachgeschoß ist jetzt ein privates Luxus-Apartment.

Architecte: Schulze & Weaver, construit en 1929. Hôtel et immeuble d'habitations étroit, dans le genre romantique-élégant; la salle de bal sous le toit est aujourd'hui un appartement de luxe particulier.

Graham House
22 East 89th Street/
Madison Avenue

Architect: unknown, built around 1892. Of note is the gigantic Romanesque-revival style portal.

Architekt: unbekannt, um 1892 erbaut. Bemerkentwertes gigantisches Portal im neoromanischen Stil.

Architecte: inconnu, construit vers 1892. Remarquable portail gigantesque dans le style néo-roman.

The following publications were of particular help with research:

Bei der Recherche waren folgende Publikationen besonders hilfreich:

Les publications suivantes ont été particulièrement utiles lors des recherches:

JACKSON, KENNETH T. (ED.): *The Encyclopedia of New York City*, Yale University Press, New Haven and London, The New York Historical Society, New York, 1955

WILLENSKY, ELLIOT, AND NORVAL WHITE, NEW YORK CHAPTER, AMERICAN INSTITUTE OF ARCHITECTS: *AIA Guide to New York City*, Harcourt Brace Jovanovich Publishers, San Diego, New York, London, 1988

Acknowledgements / Danksagung / Remerciements

This book is dedicated to my friend Anna Golin, the cosmopolitan
Swiss architect and designer, my mentor and critic.
I am particularly grateful to the photographer Marianne Princess
zu Sayn-Wittgenstein-Sayn. It was she who in the 80s first
inspired me with her infectious enthusiasm for New York.
For their friendly cooperation, I would like to thank the editors-in-
chief of "Elle Decor" USA, "House & Garden", "New York Times
Magazine" and "W" in New York, "InStyle Magazine" in Los
Angeles, "Tatler" in London and "Architektur & Wohnen" in
Hamburg. Their magazines were the first to print some of the
productions published here.
Last but not least my thanks go to Dr Angelika Taschen, the
editor, and Benedikt Taschen, the publisher of this book for their
kind cooperation.

Beate Wedekind